Netball Practices and Training

A Practical Guide for Players and Coaches

Anita Navin

THE CROWOOD PRESS

First published in 2012 by
The Crowood Press Ltd
Ramsbury, Marlborough
Wiltshire SN8 2HR

www.crowood.com

British Library Cataloguing-in-Publication Data
A catalogue record for this book is available from the British Library.

ISBN 978 1 84797 380 1

Dedication

In memory of Julia Egan, a passionate sports fan and supporter of England Netball.

Acknowledgements

The author and publishers would like to thank the following for their help in the production of this book: Denise Egan for her expertise and knowledge in designing the chapter on Defending; Jane Lomax for her knowledge of Sport Psychology and the completion of Chapter 6; to Into Sport and Northumbria University for the photographs. Thanks also to the Into Sport Group for provision of practice diagrams, www.intosportgroup.com.

The Author and Contributors

Anita Navin is currently Head of Department for Sport Development at Northumbria University, and a member of the Coaching Advisory group with the International Federation for Netball Associations (IFNA). Anita has been involved with England Netball for over twenty-five years as a player, coach, tutor, tutor trainer, technical writer and consultant for the UK Coaching Certificate developments. Anita has coached at International level with the Northern Ireland Netball Association, assisted in the coaching at Super League level and for over ten years was a coach in the England High Performance programme. Anita has contributed to the training programmes associated with decision training in both the qualification route and short course programmes. Anita is also a commentator with the Sky Sports TV channel for the weekly televised Netball Super League programme.

Denise Egan has been coaching within the England Netball Performance Programme for over twenty-five years and is a successful World Championship and Commonwealth Games netball coach. Denise is now working in Coach Education and is currently a tutor for the UKCC Level 3 alongside another role as a National Selector.

Jane Lomax is currently co-ordinating a Sports Coaching and Physical Education degree programme at the University of Chichester, and is a coach education tutor and assessor for all levels of qualifications in Netball. Jane has over twenty-five years' coaching experience, including work with National Talent League teams and the English and British Universities squads. Jane also has over twenty years' experience as a sports psychologist, including five years with the England netball squads.

Typeset by Phoenix Typesetting, Auldgirth, Dumfriesshire

Printed and bound in Singapore by Craft Print International Ltd

CONTENTS

INTRODUCTION

The implementation of decision-training by a coach will ensure that a performer can cope with the pressure of competition because they will have experienced a range of practice scenarios that simulate the competitive environment. Decision-training will build confidence and enhance the cognitive processes of a performer by developing attention, problem-solving skills and anticipatory components. Through a decision-training approach, the player will learn to make decisions under the many conditions encountered in the sport.

The Benefits of Decision-Training Practices
* Develop a capacity to anticipate forthcoming events.
* Attend to critical cues.
* Practice in selecting the best response from memory.
* Develop selective attention and learn to focus on the correct cues.
* Make effective decisions in pressure situations.

Decision-training practices provide the opportunity for physical and cognitive capacities to be developed, which will ultimately result in greater performance gains when compared to traditional closed practices.

Skilled performance is often measured by the consistency in the response demonstrated by a performer. Skilled performance will display the following features:

* Task-orientated and goal-directed.
* Involve some neurological activity and cognitive processes.
* Is dependent upon practice and learning.
* Can be modified and regulated to adapt to varying contexts.

Skilled performance therefore has a specific objective and purpose, incorporates decision-making, requires a commitment to practice and can be modified to suit internal conditions (such as effort) and external ones (such as opponents).

In every sport an individual will be forced to make a range of decisions prior to the execution of a pass, for example: When and where to pass the ball? What weight of pass is required? What type of pass to execute? The decisions requiring attention relate closely to what are called 'perceptual factors'. For example, an attacking player in any invasion game (such games have three common aims, which are to gain and regain possession, create space to move into another teams half and finally to score more points than the other team to win the game) would consider the following factors prior to executing a movement in order to free themselves from an opponent:

* The free space and where to move.
* Timing: when to move and when to break free.
* Speed and pace required to free oneself.
* Direction and angle of the movement.

This processing of information can be broken down into stages and this is outlined below:

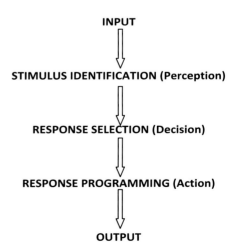

INPUT

↓

STIMULUS IDENTIFICATION (Perception)

↓

RESPONSE SELECTION (Decision)

↓

RESPONSE PROGRAMMING (Action)

↓

OUTPUT

The stages of processing relating to the decision-making between the input (individual receives environmental information) and output (final action) are identified as: Stimulus Identification, Response Selection and Response Programming. Within the Stimulus identification stage an individual will analyse the environmental information using their senses, that is, auditory, vision and kinaesthetic. At this stage the performer will assimilate the information and detect movement, speed and direction of any objects or opponents. At the conclusion of this initial stage, the performer will have a clear overview of the information presented for the second stage of Response Selection.

Given that the nature of the environment has been determined, the performer must make a decision as to what, if any, action is required. If a response is required, the individual must now select an appropriate movement from a range stored in memory from previous experiences. For example, a basketball player may have a choice to pass or dribble; given enough space in front and no approaching defender, the player would choose the latter.

Once this decision has been made, the information is passed through to the Response Programming stage. Here, the plan of action is formed and through a range of cognitive processes the muscles are directed to contract in a correct sequence, with appropriate force and timing. The output stage represents the end result of information processing.

Decision-making is governed by a performer's reaction time and this is best defined as the time gap between the presentation of the stimulus and the start of the response. Reaction time can therefore serve as a time measure of the three stages outlined above. The shortest reaction time appears when there is only one stimulus and one response (Simple Reaction Time). However, when numerous stimuli are presented with several possible responses (Choice Reaction Time), this increases the time taken to react. Thus a performer should aim to deceive their opponent by increasing the number of actions, for example, using a variety of shots in badminton with similar preparatory stages would effectively delay the opponent's information processing.

A coach must therefore apply this notion of information processing to ensure that the practices planned for a session incorporate opportunities to make decisions in environments offering a range of stimuli at the input stage. Vickers (1996) accounts for two distinct methods of coaching. The first method, known as the Traditional or Technical method of coaching, is outlined as possessing the following features:

* Technical and physical emphasis.
* Progressing from simple to complex practices.
* Large amounts of coach feedback.
* Repetitive (blocked) practice.
* Low levels of questioning.
* Low levels of athlete detection and correction of errors.
* Low levels of performer cognitive effort.

A coach utilizing this method would only implement competitive situations as the season progressed, therefore the result would be to produce a well-drilled and successful performer early in practice but one who would fail under the pressure of competition.

The second method is the decision-making approach, in which the following features are identified by Vickers:

* High levels of cognitive effort.
* Combined skill (random) practice.
* Competition scenarios.
* High levels of questioning.
* Reduced and delayed feedback.
* Athlete detection and correction of errors.
* Use of video feedback.
* High variability in activities.

A coach employing this method will witness an increased amount of error in the early stages of practice, but the performer will retain information more effectively and perform to a higher level later in the season or phase. The performer is equipped to cope when novel and challenging situations are presented in competition as a result of the independence advocated in this coaching method. It is therefore essential that a coach constantly reflects upon the methods employed within their coaching programmes. Coaching sessions should be planned to allow a performer to experience:

* Game contexts providing the 'big picture' and game scenarios.
* Modified, simulated and real contexts.
* Combined sessions of technical and physical skills.

DECISION-TRAINING METHODS

The chapters of this book offer practices that will engage a player in a range of game-related activities. Practice design is vital and a coach should ensure that decision-training practices utilize random and variable practice design. This book also outlines the importance of questioning as a decision-training tool.

Random Practice

Practices using this approach are designed to combine a range of skills from the same sport within game-like practices. Vickers (1996) refers to the skills selected as 'smart combinations' and two or three skills are placed within the same practice along with inter-linked tactical information.

Often a coach will plan logical progressions, moving from simple to more complex practices following the philosophy that the fundamental skills must be mastered prior to more advanced ones being introduced. This practice design is referred to as 'blocked practice' and is characterized by repetitions of the same skill. However, random design, when combining safe practice, decision-making and smart combinations of skills, is deemed most appropriate in terms of psychological and physical preparation. The differences between blocked and random practice are outlined in the following scenario.

Scenario: A coach is planning a practice session for three passing skills (A = the chest pass, B = the shoulder pass and C = the bounce pass); if this were to be delivered adopting a blocked design each skill would be practised in isolation and would involve repeated rehearsal of the same skill until competence is achieved. If the coach adopts a random practice design there would be no particular order to the practice, so it would incorporate the execution of the different passes as a smart combination. Therefore:

*   Blocked practice = repeated rehearsal of the same task, for example; the chest pass (AAAAAAAAAAAA).
*   Random practice = no particular order to the practice of different tasks, for example; the chest, shoulder and bounce pass in no particular order (ABCAACBBCABC).

Variable Practice

A coach will strive to incorporate a range of practices that offer variations of the same skill, for example when sprinting to get free from an opponent the coach should ensure this can be achieved using a variety of directions and in varying amounts of space and locations on the court. Varying the conditions impacts upon the attention and cognitive effort demanded for each repetition. When using this design a performer will

engage in a great deal of problem-solving and will be constantly retrieving information from their memory.

In a blocked practice design the performer would practise the sprint to get free within the same conditions. Here the performer moves into an automatic state and simply executes the movement with very little thought and planning. The resultant impact of such a practice design is a performer who moves into a mindless state after the first two or three repetitions. In the short term, the effects of blocked practice are higher, but over time the benefits of random practice will be significantly greater.

Questioning

Each of the practices within this book offers an exemplar question that a coach could pose to her players. By use of this empowering approach, the players' thought processes and cognitive efforts will be stimulated each session.

If a coach selects to reduce or delay feedback, it is of paramount importance that a questioning approach is implemented. The impact of this questioning approach will prompt greater decision-making and encourage the performer to use kinaesthetic awareness to review their performance. Questions can vary in the amount of cognitive demand placed upon the respondent. Divergent or open-ended questions are most effective in promoting decision-making and are best described as questions that do not have a straight 'yes' or 'no' answer. Questions that begin with 'What?' or 'Tell me about?' prompt the respondent to offer an account of a situation or event and to apply their knowledge to their answer. The following guide is useful for any individual using a questioning approach:

*   Questions should focus attention.
*   Questions should invite enquiry.
*   Questions should assess knowledge and understanding.
*   Questions should develop self- and peer-assessment skills.
*   Questions must be planned in advance and relate to the practice or session focus.

Some of the common errors in questioning are a result of: convergent questions being posed; poor vocabulary and lack of clarity; allowing mass calling out of the answers; focusing on the same performer to respond; not allowing time for an individual to think and answer; ignoring answers; and intolerant responses to incorrect answers.

There is a staged process for any coach to adhere to

when planning a session involving decision-training. Initially the coach should identify the game situation and be knowledgeable about the decisions a player would need to make to be successful, for example when the team is competing in a forthcoming game against opponents who make fast transitions from defence to attack following a gain in possession. Here the coach must identify the decisions to be made, which would include: What method of defence should be employed on losing possession? Where should each player position given the location of the ball carrier? Which players should be tracked closely? Each game-related decision will employ one or more of the following cognitive skills:

* **Anticipation:** the ability to predict what will occur when preparing to execute a skill.
* **Attention:** the ability to select the correct cue from the many available before and as the action is performed.
* **Focus and concentration:** the ability to select continuously the correct cues and not be distracted by irrelevant events over an extended period of time.
* **Pattern recognition:** the ability to detect the ball and player movement while on the move in tactical plays.
* **Memory retrieval:** the ability to find the best solutions in memory, given the ever-changing conditions in the game.
* **Problem-solving:** the ability to transform a given situation into a goal situation when no obvious solution is available.
* **Decision-making:** the ability to make the best choice between a set of alternatives.

Next, a coach should be able to select the correct practice to train the decision-making process, confident that they fully understand the relevant cognitive skill(s) from the list above. Effective questioning coupled with either random (smart combinations) or variable (smart variations) practice design will promote a suitable environment for learning. This book offers a range of variable and random practice designs that also focus on a selection of cognitive skills.

GAME PRINCIPLES FOR ATTACK AND DEFENCE

A competent player will not only be able to perform the technical skills to a high standard, but will also be aware of the principles of attack and defence advo-

cated in netball. This book will offer an opportunity for a coach to develop a player to perform according to the game principles:

Attacking Principles
* To score goals.
* To make use of the straight line.
* To be ball-side.
* To move the ball fast and flat.
* To create and penetrate space.
* To give the ball carrier options.
* To make use of the square ball to a player on the overlap run.

Scoring goals is the aim of two players in netball, namely the goal shooter and goal attack. Both shooters should strive to receive the ball in order to shoot in a high-per centage shooting area of the circle, which for most shooters is the mid- or inner-range shooting area. Each shooter must practise frequently and possess the skill of shooting under pressure, hence game-related pressures should be simulated in practice sessions. The direct route to goal is in a straight line, so all players should be encouraged to utilize this route, while also ensuring that the diagonal pass is avoided. Being ball-side of an opponent means that the defence will find it more difficult to intercept a pass and the ball can be distributed without passing over a defender, hence it is a safer pass. Players should ensure that there are three options always available, preferably two forward options and one coming from behind on the overlap run. The latter is often the third choice, but can open up the court and can also prevent attacking players being drawn too far up the court. Creating and penetrating space is also a key principle and all players should work to achieve a balanced court and prevent overcrowding in one area:

Defending Principles
* To gain possession.
* To be ball-side.
* To force an error (apply pressure).
* To limit options.
* To deny and close down space.
* To make use of the square ball to a player on the overlap run.

The defending principles will obviously offer opportunities for a player to counteract the work of the attack and a coach should therefore integrate these in decision-training practices. Gaining possession is the main priority of any defending player and using cognitive skills will ensure greater success in this role. The defender must strive to place pressure on the attacker and gain a ball-side position so as to force a higher and more lofted pass. By being between the ball and the player, the defender is given a prime opportunity to gain an interception. Forcing an error and pressurizing the attacking players is achieved through communication and teamwork, with all defending players working towards a set strategy, for example, forcing all players wide, inwards or up the court. Through communication within the defending team or unit the opposition can be marked closely and placed under intense pressure, often leaving the defence with a clear indication of where the ball will be distributed.

The game principles should be an essential feature of any decision-training practices in netball. A player who can execute skills with an efficient technique, apply the principles in attack and defence and cope with the pressure of the competition environment will undoubtedly have been exposed to the most productive training environment.

In summary, decision-training as a coaching method will enhance a performer's desire to take responsibility for their own learning and development. Educating others regarding the importance of this approach is vital, as initially performance improvement will be much slower when compared to the use of more traditional methods. However, traditional methods do not engage the performer in thought processes and often puts them into a mindless and automatic state of performance that is not reflective of the competitive environment. A coach should develop methods to engage a player fully in the cognitive processes linked to performance in order to promote long-term gains and retention. This book offers 180 practices from a range of contexts in the game of netball and with the progression notes for each one there is scope for a coach to have more than 500 decision-training practices at their disposal. Each practice offers examples of questions to pose.

Key		Thrower	T_{number}
Player movement	⟹	Thrower with ball	T_x
Ball movement	- - - - -▶	Catcher	C_{number}
Area markers	- - - - - - -	Feeder	F_{number}
Centre of space	- -+- -	Cones	▲▲▲▲▲
Player	P_{number}	Team 1	X
Player with ball	P_x	Team 2	O
Defender	D_{number}	2 players	XX
Cone movement	◀·······▶	Bibs	▱▱
Cone gates	●- - - - -●	Tennis ball	X

NB: Spot markers are often used instead of cones.

CHAPTER I

DECISION-TRAINING PRACTICES FOR USE IN THE WARM-UP

PLANNING THE SESSION AND THE WARM-UP

A successful coaching session is one that is planned and relates closely to the overall annual plan. It goes without saying that those coaches who fail to plan will undoubtedly plan to fail. The coach must always adopt a player-centred approach and, in doing this, ensure that the needs of the players are put first, rather than the activity, parents and the coach's own goals and ambitions. Each individual (whatever their age, ability or disability) in a session must be viewed as an individual with unique needs, interests and goals. A coach who possesses the knowledge of how a session should be structured will be able to deliver one that contains appropriate progression and ultimately achieves its purpose.

> **The Content of a Session**
> * Introduction and warm-up.
> * Skill-development section.
> * Competitive element (small-sided or full game).
> * Cool-down and conclusion.

A STEP-BY-STEP GUIDE TO SESSION PLANNING

Session Goals

It is essential that the coach states clearly what the players should have achieved by the end of a session and that the intentions are stated as session goals on the plan. There should not be too many goals to achieve and the goals must be measurable, for example, to be able to execute a shoulder pass at the appropriate time.

A coach should use the SMART acronym to ensure that the goals set are accurate. All goals should be:

* **S**pecific: for example, to use a change of direction to get free at the appropriate time.
* **M**easurable: for example, always to look to pass forwards for the first option.
* **A**djustable: by monitoring progress throughout the session, the coach should be able to see if the goal is not achievable and should make any necessary adjustments.
* **R**ealistic: a goal should be challenging but within reach for a performer.
* **T**ime-based: goals should be set for the session (short-term) and they should link closely to the intermediate- and long-term goals for the players.

A coach should also set personal goals for the session that relate to their own coaching skills and performance. This will allow a coach to continue to develop professionally by constantly reviewing their own performance.

Equipment

A coach should know what equipment is available in order to plan for the session and this should be appropriate for the group. For example, Under-eleven players will use size 4 netballs as opposed to size 5.

Duration

It is vital in the planning stages that the coach is aware of the optimum duration of the session. The length of a session should take account of the playing level and stage of development of each individual, for example a 90-minute session should be the maximum time for a potential player, whereas an open-age group player will often train for a 2-hour period. In the planning stage, a coach should ensure that the time is maximized by creating smooth transitions from one activity to another. Once the content of the session has been decided, the coach should allocate a period of time to each phase, allowing adequate transition time between activities.

Number of Players

A coach should know how many players will be at the session and also give consideration to the different ability levels, development and training ages. Any individual medical or health issues should also be considered.

Content

There are several factors that could impact upon the content of a session, for example: the stage in the season; previous performances in competition and training; lifestyle issues; and player motivation. A coach should select the practices, progressions and game activities required to achieve the session goals. Progressions should be carefully planned to ensure an appropriate increase in complexity.

It is also important to be able to adapt any practice plans should the number of participants change, for example planning for an even number and one player does not turn up. Some players may find a practice too easy or too difficult; alternative tasks or targets should therefore be prepared in advance.

For each practice, the coach should state one or two coaching points on the session plan to ensure that the participants have clear points to focus on in order to improve their performance.

Adapting an Activity

Activities will need to be adapted to suit all individuals within a session, as there may be differences in relation to ability, experience, developmental level, physiological aspects and attention span. The following are tips for adapting an activity:

* Modify equipment, for example lower the post, or use a smaller ball.
* Adapt the rules, for example, ban overhead passing in order to ensure that certain skills are practised, or shooters can only shoot from the inner area of the circle.
* Modify the practice by making the area smaller if the practice focus is on getting free from an oppo-

Turning quickly to sight all the options on attack.

nent, or increase the area if the practice has a defending focus. Increasing the number of players means that a ball carrier has more decisions to make.
* Individuals with special needs must not be neglected, for example, players with visual impairments will require a coach to use their name more frequently and using a ball with a bell inside is a useful aid. Individuals with speech or hearing impairments will need more time to convey their thoughts and the coach should encourage the use of visual cues, for example, the umpire may have a flag to raise if the whistle cannot be heard when an infringement has occurred.

Volume and Intensity
A coach must set a sufficient number of hydration breaks within the session and also ensure that participants have appropriate work-to-rest ratios. If a practice involves sprinting (for example, sprinting to receive a pass over 10m), a player must ensure that the appropriate work rate is maintained, otherwise the desired practice effect cannot be achieved. When working on a practice involving short sprints an individual on average will be able to complete between six and eight repetitions before performance levels deteriorate. This period of work should be followed by a rest period, giving time for the body to recover (work to rest = 1:2 or 1:3, depending on fitness levels).

Task and Group Management

When planning the session, a coach must ensure that all the space is used effectively and that groups have clear boundaries in which to practise. The session plan should identify the areas within which the groups will work and often a coach will use the court markings or cones to communicate the working areas to the group.

Grouping is also a key consideration when planning and a coach can group according to ability, friendship, developmental level or randomly. Ensuring that individuals are challenged in the group activities is a

paramount concern and so ability groupings may be more beneficial. A coach should vary the groupings within and between sessions to ensure that individuals are able to work with a range of players as the season progresses.

Coaching is a cyclical process, whereby the coach will plan, deliver and review each session. All stages are important and should be valued equally to ensure success.

Warm-Up

The warm-up should prepare players mentally and physically for the subsequent activities by incorporating dynamic mobility activities and ball work.

Dynamic Movement Skills for a Warm-Up
The following dynamic movement activities are examples of what should feature in the early stages of the warm-up. Once completed, the netball-specific ball work can begin.

Examples:
* Sidestepping, leading with right and left leg.
* Skipping with a low knee lift.
* Skipping with high knee lift, adding arm swings.
* Stretching the calf muscle in the lunge position and simultaneously swinging one arm in a spiral pattern, then repeating on the other leg.
* Carioca stepping followed by wide leg squats (lead left, then right leg).
* Lunging forwards in a variety of directions, while simultaneously reaching with arms in various directions.
* Ankle rolls for 10m, heel flicks for 10m, followed by two-footed jump.
* Falling start, then sprinting forwards with three quick steps; repeat.
* Performing hamstring stretch in standing position while turning trunk to either side; repeat with other leg.
* Sprinting forwards for five strides, stopping, returning backwards with diagonal step-overs to the right. Repeat, but diagonally back to the left. Repeat to complete three in each direction.

Incorporating decision-making practices within the warm-up will ensure that players are challenged mentally and physically at the outset. The principles of the game can also be integrated, which would then ensure that the theme and goals of the session are interspersed throughout.

FUNDAMENTAL MOVEMENT SKILLS

Fundamental movement skills provide the backbone for the effective execution of netball-specific skills. The movement skills are developed in the early stages of an individual's training, but should continue to be refined throughout their career. Progressive practices should initially isolate the movement aspect of any netball skill, allowing the individual an opportunity to work on their movement repertoire without the pressure of the ball being in a practice session. Effective warm-ups should integrate the movement skills relevant to the positional demands of the session and should also be relevant to the overall session goals. For example, if the session had a focus on defending, the movement skills integrated in the warm-up should include: sidestepping, jumping and changes of direction.

The key movement skills are outlined below:

Take-Off

The take-off is described as the first step required to initiate a movement, either from a moving or stationary position. A player needs to be able to execute this first step effectively so as to maximize the speed of the response to their decision to move. Working on this initial take-off step maximizes the chance of beating an opponent to the ball.

Key coaching points:
* Feet shoulder-width apart.
* Opposite arm to leg drives forwards.
* Body upright and balanced with weight over feet.
* Head up, looking ahead.
* High knee lift to initiate the take-off step.

Common errors:
* Knee lift not high enough.
* Hips not leaning forwards in the direction of the movement.
* Stepping back before going forwards.

Agility is a much needed attribute to chase a loose ball.

Sprinting

The ability to move at speed is an essential skill for netball and the ability to change pace and direction must also be trained. Players will combine an effective take-off with a sprint to ensure they move as quickly as possible through the court when on attack and defence.

Key coaching points:
* Feet shoulder-width apart.
* Keep weight on balls of feet.
* Head up and upper body upright.
* Opposite arm to leg, with arms bent at 90 degrees.
* High knee lift.

Common errors:
* Arms not synchronized with the leg action.
* Stride length too long and more than a shoulder width distance.
* Knee lift too low.

Tight man-to-man defence.

Change of Direction

A change of direction is effective when trying to deceive an opponent. The attacker moves in one direction, then stops and cuts back in another.

Key coaching points:
* Feet shoulder-width apart.
* Weight over the feet.
* Upper body balanced over the feet and upright.
* Change of direction initiated with a strong plant of the outside foot.
* Strong push-off from the outside foot to speed up the directional change, with the inside foot leading.
* Hips and shoulders turn quickly to accelerate in the new direction.

Common errors:
* Upper body dips downwards when the foot is planted to change direction.
* A long stride is used, leading into the foot plant to change direction.

* Hips are slow to turn into the direction of the movement.

Change of Pace

A change of pace is often executed to displace a defender, allowing the player to receive the ball in an uncontested space. Elite performers will use a moderate pace as the opponent tracks them through a space and then suddenly accelerate to get free. A change of pace can also be accompanied with a change of direction to outwit an opponent.

Key coaching points:
* Keep body upright, with good body balance and alignment.
* Use small steps to allow for a sudden change of pace.
* Pump the arms to accelerate.
* Keep weight over the feet when decreasing the pace.

Common errors:
* Stride length too big when increasing the pace.
* Limited use of the arms when accelerating.
* Body not balanced over the feet.
* Upper body dips when accelerating.

Jumping

Players have to jump from both stationary and moving positions, which requires jumping to be executed off one and two feet. Within the fundamentals stage, coaches should ensure that young performers experience and practise the five basic jumps, which are:

* Jumping from two feet to land on two feet.
* Jumping from one foot to land on the same foot.
* Jumping from two feet to land on one foot.
* Jumping from one foot to land on the other foot.
* Jumping from one foot to land on two feet.

Netball is an aerial game with several passes being caught in the air, therefore jumping is a vital movement skill for a player receiving a pass, or when defending a high ball. There is also a need for players to jump and extend forwards to take a ball at speed.

Coaching points for jumping upwards:
* Use a two-footed base where possible.
* Feet shoulder-width apart.
* Lower the hips but keep the body upright.
* Arms swing back and vigorously upwards.

* Maintain a straight body position in the air.

Coaching points for jumping forwards:
* Bend knees, lower hips but keep body upright.
* Swing arms, lowering and driving the body forwards.
* Keep head up.

Common errors:
* Limited arm movement in the direction of the jump.
* Hips do not lower sufficiently for the upwards jump.
* Knees are not flexed on take-off.

Landing

The ability to land is an essential skill required to accompany a jump, particularly when considering the footwork rule applied in netball. Landing effectively is crucial in terms of preventing injury and a coach will always spend a great deal of time on developing this technique.

Key coaching points:
* Knees flexed and ankles slightly flexed on impact.
* Land on the balls of the feet.
* Keep upper body upright, abdominals tight and head upright.
* If landing on one foot, bring the other down as quickly as possible to ensure balance and control.

Common errors:
* Landing on the heels or flat-footed.
* Not flexing the knees.
* Body leaning forwards over the feet.

Sidestep

The use of a sidestep is an essential movement skill that will enhance a player's ability to get free, move around and also track an opponent when defending. The use of a sidestep will allow circle players to move in various directions in an attempt to outwit an opponent within a confined space. Defending through all areas of the court involves tracking a player from in front and often the lateral movement means a sidestep may be used.

Key coaching points:
* Keep on the balls of the feet.
* Head up.
* Knees slightly flexed with the trunk upright.
* Feet should remain shoulder-width apart.
* Weight should be balanced over the feet.

Common errors:
* Feet beyond shoulder width.
* Weight falls over the outside foot.

Turning in the Air

Jumping and landing are the essential skills supporting the ability to turn in the air. A player will use a turn in the air to ensure that on landing she faces the direction of play and the attacking goal. The ball carrier in netball has only 3 seconds in which to make a decision and pass or shoot. If a player can jump and turn in the air before landing this will allow more time to observe the options available and make the appropriate decision. Turning in the air removes the need to pivot after landing to face the direction of play.

Key coaching points:
* Use the coaching points for jumping.
* After take-off begin to initiate the turn with the head, shoulders and hips turning.
* Keep the body upright and abdominals tight.
* Maintain the balanced body position on landing.

Common errors:
* Not turning the hips after take-off and initiating the turn early.

The movement skills outlined in this chapter will support the development of all netball-specific skills.. The ability to move efficiently requires effective technique accompanied with the required level of fitness. All of the movement skills outlined require good physical conditioning and players must work hard to ensure they are fast, strong and powerful.

PRACTICE: QUAD BALL NUMBERS: TEN TO FOURTEEN

The ball is passed around in groups of four and each group must move through all areas within the defined space.

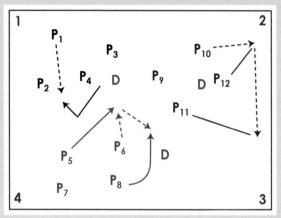

Practice Outcomes

* To use a single and double lead to receive the ball.

* To remain ball-side in relation to the floating defenders.

* To balance the space with the other players in the group.

* To communicate with the group to locate the next available space in which to move.

Task/Group Organization

Use a third of the court and four spaces are defined.

Three groups should be allocated to a space (fours).

Players should move into each area and make five passes before locating another space in which to move.

Defenders remain in one of the spaces and float to try to get ball-side.

Work for 30 seconds.

Progressions and Differentiation

Defenders can pick up one on one to pressurize individual players.

The space can be made smaller to place the attack under more pressure.

Potential Question to Pose

When would you use a double lead to receive the ball?

(Answer: When close to a defender to get ball side or near a sideline.)

PRACTICE: PAIRS PASS PUT DOWN NUMBERS: EIGHT TO TWELVE

Players work in pairs passing a tennis ball as they move around the defined area and on the command 'change', place the ball down and collect another.

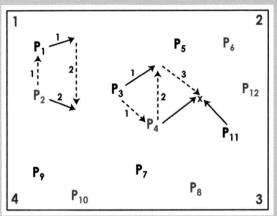

Practice Outcomes

* To use a range of movement skills to move around the area (sidestep, back pedal, running).

* To balance the space with the other players in the group.

* To communicate with a partner and move to the free space.

Task/Group Organization

Use a third of the court.

Six pairs should be allocated to a space.

Players should begin the practice by ensuring that the space is balanced.

Work for 30–45 seconds.

Progressions and Differentiation

Players must touch a line before they retrieve another ball.

Two balls per pair – one netball and one tennis ball.

Potential Question to Pose

What is a player's role when their partner is back-pedalling into a space?

(Answer: To provide the eyes and communicate if a player is close by.)

PRACTICE: TOUCH DOWN
NUMBERS: EIGHT

Four players are on attack and four on defence – the attacking four must successfully pass the ball to the other line.

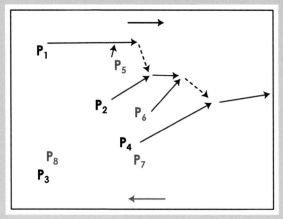

Practice Outcomes

* To pass the ball in a group of four to the far line.

* To receive ball-side in relation to the defenders.

* To always have two offers for the ball carrier.

* To use a square pass if the defence prevents an attacker moving ahead and on ball-side.

Task/Group Organization

Use a third of the court and ensure players work up and down the court.

The attack has three chances to achieve a touchdown (ball placed on the line).

3v3 set-up (P1–4 are the attackers).

The team who were on attack become defenders after each touchdown or break in play for the attack.

Work for 30–45 seconds.

Progressions and Differentiation

Add more players to a space with a higher ability group.

Players have a set number of passes to achieve in 30 seconds (for example, twelve).

Potential Question to Pose

How can two attacking players deceive the defence?

(Answer: One player can make a move to pull the defence in one direction and the other attacker then moves to the open space.)

PRACTICE: BIB GRAB
NUMBERS: TWELVE

Four players in each team who compete to claim the most bibs at their corner.

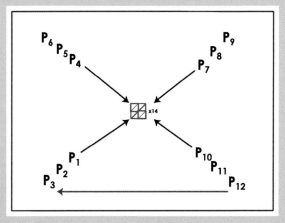

Practice Outcomes

*   To execute a sprint and change of direction while competing to collect bibs.

*   To use effective decision making to select where to collect a bib from (either centre or a team area).

*   To use peripheral vision to sight potential movement to your own team area and counteract this by collecting a bib from the opponent's area.

Task/Group Organization

Use a third of the court and place fourteen bibs in the centre.

The teams must collect two bibs from the centre and then players can either collect from the centre or a team area.

Only one team member can move at any one time and must have placed the bib in the team area prior to the next player moving.

Work for 90 seconds.

Progressions and Differentiation

Allow two players to be moving from each team.

Players can elect to not collect a bib but restrict and delay the movement of another team for 10 seconds.

Potential Question to Pose

What is your strategy against a team with three more bibs than you and 30 seconds to go?

(Answer: Must take bibs from their team area and move to the nearest teams for collecting bibs.)

PRACTICE: GATEWAY NUMBERS: EIGHT TO SIXTEEN

A player defends a space between two cones (a gate) and the attacking players are trying to move through as many 'gates' as possible.

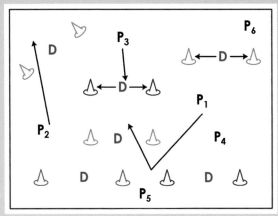

Practice Outcomes

* To use a range of movement skills to outwit the defender and move through the gate (sprint, change of direction, sidestep, change of pace).

* To use peripheral vision to locate the next available gate.

* To look ahead and plan the next route to a gate.

Task/Group Organization

Use a third of the court eight (twelve cones).

Six gates with defence and six attacking players.

Gates should be 5m apart.

Defence should sidestep only between the gates.

Work for 30–45 seconds.

Progressions and Differentiation

The distance of the gates can be reduced.

Defence can restrict by moving forwards, backwards and sideways.

Potential Question to Pose

What methods can be used to outwit the defender at the gate?

(Answers: Use a fast change of direction, sell the dummy or fake or deceive by moving to one gate and quickly change.)

PRACTICE: THINK TANK
NUMBERS: TEN TO FOURTEEN

There are static throwers and players who move within the defined area to receive a pass.

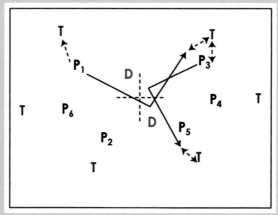

Practice Outcomes

* To use a range of movement skills to move through the centre of the defined space and receive a pass (sprint, change of direction, sidestep, change of pace).

* To use peripheral vision and read off the front player to locate the next available thrower.

* To negotiate the centre space with other attackers using a range of movement skills.

Task/Group Organization

Use a third of the court.

Six static throwers/six attackers and two floating defence in the centre area.

The centre areas can be defined by spot markers.

Each player must receive and pass back to a thrower.

Prior to receiving a pass the attacker must move through the centre area.

Work for 30–45 seconds.

Progressions and Differentiation

The defence can move anywhere in the space and use all stages of defence.

Throwers may opt to pass to each other if a suitable option is not available.

Potential Question to Pose

How can the throwers support the attacking players?

(Answer: By communicating when they are available to pass and by making eye contact with the player to whom they intend to pass.)

PRACTICE: FREE SPACE
NUMBERS: FOUR

Four players move within an area that has five spaces defined.

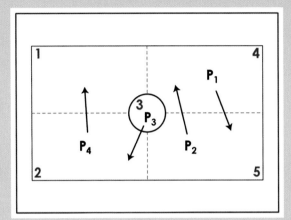

Practice Outcomes

* To use their vision to move into a free space.

* To change of pace and direction.

* To use peripheral vision and read off the front player to locate the next available space.

* To see the whole space.

Task/Group Organization

Use a third of the court.

Define the area into five spaces, or ensure there is always one more space in relation to the number of players in the area.

Players can only spend up to 3 seconds in a space.

Work for 30 seconds.

Progressions and Differentiation

Defence can be added to two areas to track the attackers and attempt to delay them for more than 3 seconds.

Players must execute a different method of getting free in each space prior to moving on.

Potential Question to Pose

When moving in this practice what should the player have in their vision?

(Answer: Should be able to see all players and the whole space.)

PRACTICE: THINK TANK TRAIL
NUMBERS: TWELVE

Players move within the space and pass to a thrower and move to receive a pass from another.

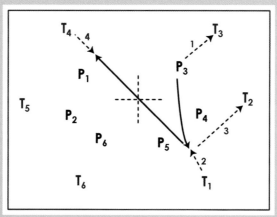

Practice Outcomes

* To pass and go, using a change of direction to sight a free thrower.

* To accelerate through the centre of the area, using a sprint and change of direction when negotiating others.

* To encourage the throwers to communicate and make eye contact with a potential attacker who is in a position to receive a pass.

Task/Group Organization

Use a third of the court.

The number of static throwers should equal the number of players moving.

Players start with the ball and must not receive a pass from the thrower to whom they distributed the ball.

Work for 30 seconds (see P3 above).

Progressions and Differentiation

Players must move to an opposite side to receive the ball, encouraging more movement.

Defence could be added and could use a range of defence – tight one to one, zone the space or mark the ball carrier.

Potential Question to Pose

What cues should a thrower be picking up about the players moving?

(Answer: How fast they move, their ball-handling ability, for example dominant on the right or left.)

PRACTICE: CONE CROSS
NUMBERS: FOUR TO SIX

Players move around the space and relocate cones to a new spot.

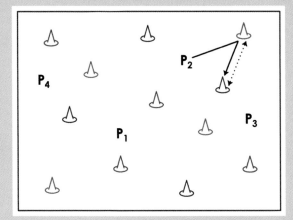

Practice Outcomes

* To balance the space they are working in as a group.

* To use a range of movement skills to move around the space (sprint, change of direction and pace).

Task/Group Organization

Use a third of the court.

Sixteen cones (four of each colour).

Player 2 in the diagram selects a green cone and moves it to the place where the blue cone is located and vice versa.

Two coloured cones interchange positions each time.

Work for 30 seconds.

Progressions and Differentiation

Players must move a cone to an opposite area, covering more space.

If a player is tagged by another player, the cone must be returned to the original space – players score a point for each interchange.

Potential Question to Pose

When a player is interchanging the cones, what should be in their vision?

(Answer: Where the other players are and which cone is free; if scoring and tagging a player should know the whereabouts of the dominant players.)

PRACTICE: COLOUR CHANGE NUMBERS: TWO

Players work in pairs and the player must travel to three different-coloured cones before receiving a pass.

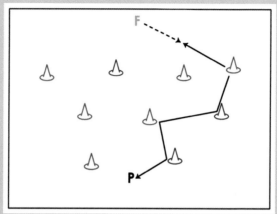

Practice Outcomes

* To use a range of movement skills to move around the space (sprint, change of direction and pace).

* To not follow the same pathway as the previous player.

* To receive a fast, flat pass from the feeder.

Task/Group Organization

Use a third of the court/in pairs.

Nine cones (three of each colour).

Thrower to position outside of the coned area.

Player moves to three coloured cones before receiving a pass from their thrower (not the same colour in succession).

Work for 30 seconds.

Progressions and Differentiation

Players must use a range of attacking moves at each cone, for example roll, feint and so on.

Players must integrate some leads to the back space.

Player could travel to two cones (easier).

Potential Question to Pose

What cues should the thrower attend to when preparing to pass?

(Answer: Know when the player is leaving the third cone, pass as the player approaches the space to receive, know how fast the receiver is.)

PRACTICE: TEAM TAG
NUMBERS: TWELVE TO SIXTEEN

Players are in two teams and each team is trying to move to the shooting circle at the opponent's end to score a goal.

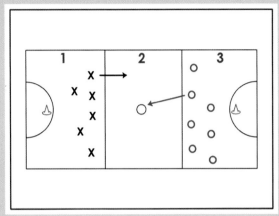

Practice Outcomes

* To use a range of strategies to outwit the opponents in order to reach the goal circle.

* To aim as a team to score the most goals within the time allocated.

* To use a range of movement skills to move around the space (sprint, change of direction and pace).

Task/Group Organization

Use a full court with a ball in each shooting circle.

Two teams have a home base area where they cannot be tagged (for example, the 'x' team has a home base in area 1).

Players can move as they wish to try to get to the opposing shooting circle to score.

If tagged, the player must return to the home base before moving again.

Progressions and Differentiation

Set a time restriction of 1 minute to try to score (harder).

Score points for getting into the opponent's home base area (easier).

Potential Question to Pose

How can a team use three or more players at once to outwit the opponents?

(Answer: Two players move in opposite directions and try to pull the defence, which may open up space for the other.)

PRACTICE: THE RUNNER
NUMBERS: TWELVE TO SIXTEEN

**Players are in two teams and a member of one team starts as the
'runner' and must try to reach the goal line in the opponent's area.**

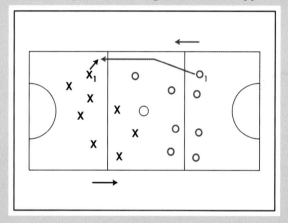

Practice Outcomes

* To use a range of strategies to outwit the opponents in order to reach the goal line.

* To use the differing strengths of the team to outwit the opposition.

* To use a sprint and change of direction when negotiating the opposition.

Task/Group Organization

Use a full court area.

The nominated first runner must try to get to the goal line before they are tagged. The person who tags becomes the runner with a chance to now get to the goal line.

Teams score a point if the runner reaches the goal line without being tagged.

Progressions and Differentiation

Set a time restriction of 1 minute to try to score.

Allocate a leader to set the team strategy.

Allow the runner to have 'two lives'.

Potential Question to Pose

What differing roles can players take within the team?

(Answer: Some players should remain in the area as defence, players with speed should attempt to be the runner and some players can set up screens.)

PRACTICE: NOUGHTS AND CROSSES
NUMBERS: SIX

Players are in two teams and must place down a bib on one of nine markers, attempting to get a full line to win.

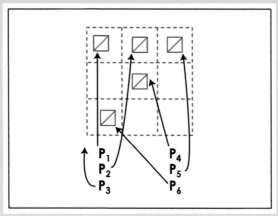

Practice Outcomes

* To pre-plan and move at speed to outwit the opposition.

* To communicate as a team to support the next mover.

* To use cognitive skills under the pressure of competition.

Task/Group Organization

Use a third area/nine markers define the grid.

Use two different-coloured sets of bibs.

Players start behind the third line and only one player from each team can move to the grid at any one time.

The team that wins will have three of their coloured bibs in a vertical, horizontal or diagonal line.

Progressions and Differentiation

The distance to sprint is reduced (easier).

Moving between cones prior to the grid.

Teams could nominate a caller who communicates the options for where to place the bib (easier).

Potential Question to Pose

What must the next player take into account before running to the grid?

(Answer: Whether two bibs are in one line for the opposition, the speed of the next runner and the direction to take when running to be ahead of them.)

PRACTICE: DOWN THE LINE
NUMBERS: NINE

Attackers versus defence in a confined space with a target of passing the ball to the opposite line.

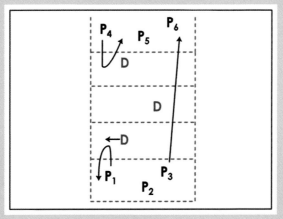

Practice Outcomes

* To pass the ball as the attack (at least three times) and try to reach the opposite line.

* To have two offers each time for the ball carrier (a short and long option where possible).

* To use the 'give and go' (sometimes called a double play) as the attack wherever possible to outwit the defence.

Task/Group Organization

Use a quarter of the court.

Each defender has a defined area in which to work.

Only one defender per area.

The attack must be ball-side of the defender.

The attacking team work the ball to the opposite line four times.

Progressions and Differentiation

The attacking team can play on from the error point and have two chances (easier).

Two defence in each area to add more pressure on the practice (harder).

Make the area smaller to pressurize the attack.

Potential Question to Pose

Why is a preliminary move used against a defender?

(Answer: To lead them away from the ball-side or the straight line, or to open up space, which may be for another player.)

PRACTICE: CLEAR THE SPACE
NUMBERS: EIGHT

Four players are passing and moving in the area, also performing clearing runs with four static throwers in each corner.

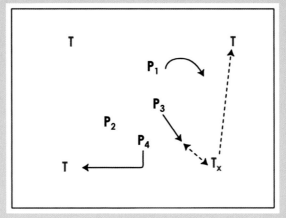

Practice Outcomes

* To be able to describe when a clearing run might be used in the game.

* To make the correct decision of whether to clear or receive a pass from the thrower.

Task/Group Organization

Use a quarter of the court – one ball.

Players pass the ball five times, then it must go to a thrower.

Throwers can pass to each other or to a player (this should be varied).

The nearest player makes a decision to clear or move to receive (thrower may elect not to pass to this player).

Progressions and Differentiation

The front player must clear and cannot receive the pass from the thrower and the throwers cannot pass between themselves (easier initially).

The player who passes to the thrower must interchange places with them.

Potential Question to Pose

When should the ball carrier not use the front mover in this practice?

(Answer: If they are moving away from the ball, or if they are running out of space ahead of them.)

PRACTICE: BEAT THE 'D'
NUMBERS: EIGHT

A defender guards the space between two cones (the gate) and the attacker must move through before moving to another area.

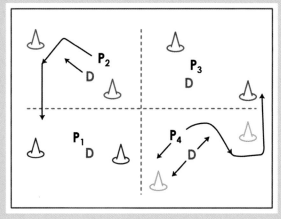

Practice Outcomes

* To be able to use a range of movement skills to outwit the defender (change of pace, direction and feint movements).

* To be able to use peripheral vision to move to the free gate in an area.

* To see as much of the space as possible at all times.

* Defenders to be able to use a range of directional movements to deny.

Task/Group Organization

Use a third of the court.

Players start in one of the four areas, scoring one point for every gate they pass through.

A player has 3 seconds to move through the gate and if unsuccessful must move to another space.

Only one player can contest with a defender at each time.

Progressions and Differentiation

Players are given a longer time period to pass through the gate, or each player chooses the time they want to allow (for example, 3, 5 or 7 seconds).

Defender movement is restricted to sidesteps only (easier).

Potential Question to Pose

When is the defender vulnerable in this practice?

(Answer: If they are recovering from a previous attacker passing through, if the current attacker moves from a different direction to the previous one.)

PRACTICE: TRACKER
NUMBERS: TWO

Players move laterally in a leader and follower style, attempting to sprint over the line.

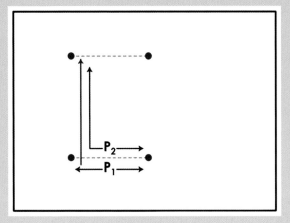

Practice Outcomes

* To show a fast take-off when sprinting against an opponent.

* To become efficient in the recovery and transition between sidestepping and sprinting forwards.

* To use good body angles if tracking to stay with the leader.

Task/Group Organization

Use a third of the court in length (three pairs could work in each third).

P1 is the leader and must sidestep for 3–10 seconds before sprinting through the cones at the opposite line.

Player 2 aims to catch player 1.

Players should rotate positions as leader or follower and three repetitions each is one workload before rest.

Progressions and Differentiation

Players are given a longer time period to pass through the gate, or each player chooses the time they want to allow (for example, 3, 5 or 7 seconds).

Defender movement is restricted to sidesteps only.

Potential Question to Pose

What should the leader quickly assess in the follower to help subsequent repetitions?

(Answer: If they are faster on the transition when sidestepping to the left.)

PRACTICE: INTERCHANGE NUMBERS: SIXTEEN

Working in groups of four players, in a space and execute double leads; on the command 'change' one player must switch to another group.

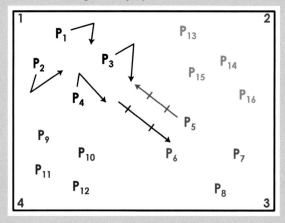

Practice Outcomes

* To be able to work on the double lead, showing an efficient change of direction.

* Each group to be able to use peripheral vision and balance the space.

* Each group to be able to communicate effectively when interchanging between players.

Task/Group Organization

Use half of the court and four groups in the area.

Players all work for 30 seconds and execute a range of double leads, moving in a range of directions each time.

On the command 'change' one player must move to another group.

Progressions and Differentiation

Players are given two directional leads to practise (for example, up to go back or left to go forwards).

To add more decision-making activity, two players should interchange to different groups.

Potential Question to Pose

What communication may occur between players who are on the interchange?

(Answer: First player to reach a new group will reduce options for others to move to so these players could call to each other.)

PRACTICE: SQUARE INTERCHANGE
NUMBERS: NINE

Players move around the area using a variety of foot patterns and on the call 'change', must move through the area to the opposite line.

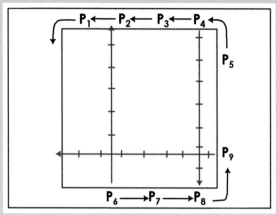

Practice Outcomes

* To be able to use a range of movement skills relative to their position played (for example, defence use sidesteps, some directional changes around the area, attackers some diagonal movement and so on) around the area.

* To achieve a good upright body position when negotiating others and moving through the area.

Task/Group Organization

Use a third of the court.

Players move clockwise and can execute movements in varying directions off the line other than backwards.

A leader in the group could call change.

Players should try to cross the area to the opposite line in 3 seconds.

Progressions and Differentiation

Players must change the direction of the outside movement after every call of 'change'.

To add more difficulty, players could move to the opposite line and return.

Potential Question to Pose

What considerations should a player make when moving across the area to the opposite line?

(Answer: Where the space is or are there players all on one side of the area as they are moving around.)

PRACTICE: INTERCHANGE CONTEST
NUMBERS: EIGHT TO SIXTEEN

Two teams move around the area using a variety of foot patterns and on the call 'change', the attack try to move to the opposite line against defence.

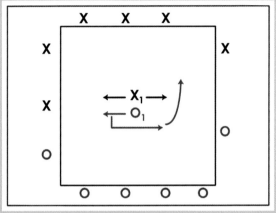

Practice Outcomes

* To look for spaces when moving through the area.

* To evaluate the strength of the defence as a unit as individuals and know what works when crossing the area.

* To attempt, as the defence, to deny space to the attacker, force wide and restrict their forward movement.

Task/Group Organization

Use a third of the court.

Players move clockwise and can execute movements in varying directions off the line other than backwards.

Players should try to cross the area to the opposite line in 3 seconds.

After 10 seconds all players move out of the area to a line.

Progressions and Differentiation

So as to reduce the challenge for the attack there could be fewer defenders, for example 8v4.

For an added attacking challenge, the space could be reduced in size.

Potential Question to Pose

What skills are important when moving towards a defender?

(Answer: Change of direction and deception will be useful.)

PRACTICE: FREE CONE
NUMBERS: FIVE

Players move in the space together and find a free cone.

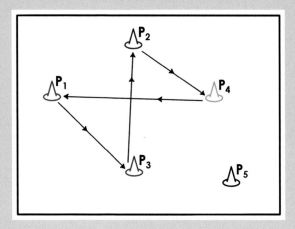

Practice Outcomes

* To look for a free cone when moving through the area.

* All players to see each other and work on their sprint and change of direction.

* To read off the front player.

Task/Group Organization

Groups of five and two groups per third.

Each player in the group places a cone in the space approximately 5m apart.

Players move to as many cones as possible in 30 seconds.

Progressions and Differentiation

To increase the challenge, players must move to a different-coloured cone.

Add a floating defender in the space to pressure the movement of the players.

Potential Question to Pose

What makes an effective change of direction at the cone?

(Answer: Pushing off on the outside foot, fast hip turn in the direction of the next movement and upper body upright.)

PRACTICE: COPE WITH THE CATCHERS
NUMBERS: TWELVE

Players look to execute a double play with a static passer, whilst at the same time avoiding the 'catcher'.

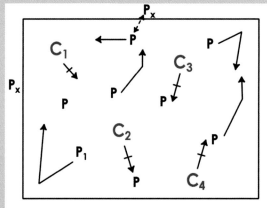

Practice Outcomes

* To look for spaces when moving through the area.

* To evaluate the strength of the defence as a unit and as individuals and know what works for them to cross the area.

* Defence to attempt to deny space to the attacker, force wide and restrict their forward movement.

Task/Group Organization

Use a third of the court, two static passers, six to eight moving players and four catchers.

Players are trying to receive and pass the ball back to a catcher as many times as possible in 30 seconds.

When tagged, the player becomes a static passer.

All players change roles.

Progressions and Differentiation

Points can be given for each successful catch and pass.

Increase the number of catchers against the players.

Potential Question to Pose

How can two players help each other against a catcher?

(Answer: Screen and get between the catcher and the player, or work together to move in differing directions to pull the catchers apart.

PRACTICE: BALL TAG
NUMBERS: TWELVE

The catchers must touch the player with the ball obeying the 3-second and footwork rule.

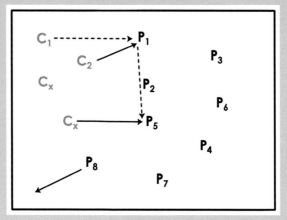

Practice Outcomes

* To use quick footwork and a change of direction.

* Catchers to pass and move at speed to reach the players.

* To make decisions in the catching role about when and where to pass.

Task/Group Organization

Use a third of the court, with four catchers in bibs and with a ball.

The catchers are given one point for each player they tag within 1 minute.

When tagged, the player becomes a catcher.

Progressions and Differentiation

Two balls can be used by the catchers.

Increase/decrease the number of catchers against the players.

Potential Question to Pose

What strategies can the catchers employ?

(Answer: Catchers move to the outside of the players to force players inwards in the space or use the double play for fast movement to a player.)

PRACTICE: TWO TO MOVE
NUMBERS: TWO

Two players are leading and balancing the space, with the front player initiating the movement.

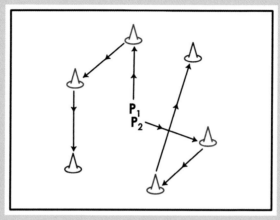

Practice Outcomes

* Two players to read off each other and attempt to balance the space

* To work to different-coloured cones while maintaining the speed and quality of the movement.

* To use body angle to sight other players at all times.

Task/Group Organization

Two or three pairs in each third and two blue, red and green cones.

If P1 moves to a red cone, P2 must do the same (for example, P1 moves to red, green and blue so P2 must copy).

Players change the lead each time and begin the practice from the position they are in after the previous repetition (in the diagram, this would be P2 leading from the blue cone).

Progressions and Differentiation

A floating defender could be placed in the practice, plus a player holding a ball to ensure the focus is forwards.

Two pairs can work in the same work space.

Potential Question to Pose

As a front mover, what is important about your movements?

(Answer: Movements must be decisive and executed with full commitment and speed.)

PRACTICE: PASSING SCRAMBLE
NUMBERS: SIXTEEN

Players pass the ball in the space and respond to varying commands.

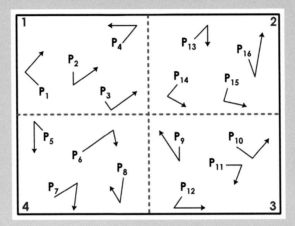

Practice Outcomes

* Four players to work to balance the space and execute fast, flat passes.

* To use a double lead each time and focus on the recovery step on the change of direction.

* To react quickly to the commands and maintain the quality of movement.

Task/Group Organization

Sixteen players can work in four areas on half the court, numbered 1–16.

Players pass the ball around for 30 seconds and respond to the coach calls, for example numbers 1, 5, 11 and 13 move to another group clockwise or players 2, 6, 10 and 14 move clockwise and defend in a 3v1.

On the whistle, resume as a four passing and work for 30–40 seconds.

Progressions and Differentiation

Coach commands will differentiate for an increased or decreased challenge (as above).

For example, call even numbers for a 2v2 in each area, or the calls are made but there is no movement between groups.

Potential Question to Pose

What cues should each player be reading in other neighbouring groups?

(Answer: Trying to remember some of the player numbers from previous commands, knowing their location in the space and who are the more dominant defenders.)

PRACTICE: COLOUR LEAD
NUMBERS: EIGHT

Players must move to a free cone, making sure all colours have been covered in each repetition.

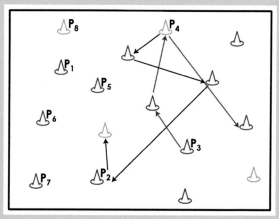

Practice Outcomes

* To use single leads to each cone and balance the space with other movers.

* To try to see the whole group or picture of movement at all times.

* To take account of player transition if two move to the same cone.

* To use decision-making in relation to where to move.

Task/Group Organization

Eight players, sixteen cones of three colours and in a third area.

Cones are placed approximately 5m apart.

Players must move to twelve cones and then rest.

If a player is ahead of another player, the back player must choose another pathway.

Progressions and Differentiation

Increase or decrease the number of cones to move to in a repetition.

There could be a golden cone where players score three points if they move to it.

Potential Question to Pose

What should you be assessing in the players you are working with?

(Answer: How fast they move, if their movements dominate one side of the area and whether faster than the other players.)

PRACTICE: COLOUR NUMBER LEAD NUMBERS: TWO

The feeder calls a sequence of numbers and colours for the player to move to before receiving the ball.

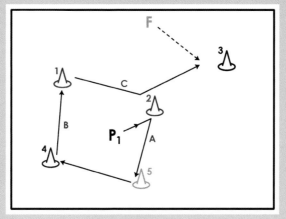

Practice Outcomes

* To work on the sprint and change of direction.

* Feeder to work on passing the ball to space and using a fast, flat pass.

* To maintain the speed of movement as the cognitive demands increase.

Task/Group Organization

Pairs and three pairs per third.

Five cones with three different colour numbers.

The feeder calls a number and a colour for the mover.

The pass is received at the final cone.

Work for four repetitions and change roles.

Progressions and Differentiation

Increase or decrease the number of calls.

Call only numbers or only colours (easier).

Call numbers followed by colours when four points are given (harder).

Potential Question to Pose

What happens to the quality of movement when the cognitive demands are overloaded?

(Answer: Movements slow down and there is some hesitation.)

PRACTICE: GATES AND COLOURS
NUMBERS: SIX

Players are moving in the area and must pass through different-coloured gates.

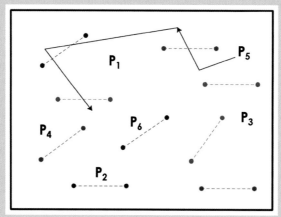

Practice Outcomes

* To work on the sprint, change of pace and change of direction.

* To build up a mental picture of where the coloured gates are located.

* To sight the free gates early and accelerate out of each change of direction.

* To be encouraged to pull wide if there are several players in one space.

Task/Group Organization

Six to eight players per third area.

Each player puts out a gate at least 5m apart.

A player may only follow another player once through a gate, which prevents a player following another.

Players must pass through six gates in one repetition.

Progressions and Differentiation

Increase or decrease the space (smaller space is more difficult).

Players must perform a range of attacking moves, for example feint, roll, half-roll and double lead.

Add floating defence (harder).

Potential Question to Pose

What makes a good attacking move?

(Answer: One showing 100 per cent commitment, leading towards the ball and on a straight line in relation to the ball carrier.)

PRACTICE: COMPETE FOR FRONT NUMBERS: TEN

As the ball is passed, the pairs compete to achieve the front position.

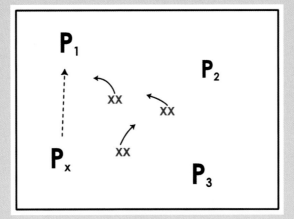

Practice Outcomes

* To develop a player's capacity to move around an attacker and gain the front position.

* To gain the ball side position and be in front of the attacker.

* To use fast feet and a change of direction to move around the other X.

* To move around the player quickly as the ball swings to the other feeders (P2 and P3).

Progressions and Differentiation

Attacker is half pace to start.

More passes between the P2 and P3 before the ball swings across to the other passing side.

Task/Group Organization

Six players in the grid in pairs and four static post players who pass and catch the ball.

Defender starts behind the Attacker.

As the ball is thrown the defender tries to get ball side and in front.

Work for 30 seconds and change.

The ball can go to P2 or P3 at any point and the defender must readjust.

Potential Question to Pose

How should the defender move around the player?

(Answer: Keep sight of the ball and try not to turn away from the attacker as this would reduce vision.)

PRACTICE: LINE TOUCH
NUMBERS: EIGHT

Each player must touch the centre of each line, defining their space with a defender restricting the movement.

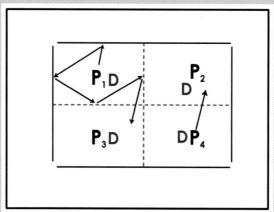

Practice Outcomes

* To work on the sprint and change of direction.

* Defence to try to force the player wide and away from the intended direction of movement.

* Defender to be able to build-up a mental picture of which lines have been touched by the player.

Task/Group Organization

Eight players maximum per third area.

Each player must touch the centre of each line before moving to the next area in a clockwise direction.

Two players could be working in one area.

The defence restricts the movement to a line for a period of 3 seconds.

Players rest when at the starting area.

Progressions and Differentiation

Increase or decrease the space (smaller space is more difficult for attacker).

Defence to restrict the movement for 3–6 seconds (more time to restrict means more pressure for the attacker).

Potential Question to Pose

Describe two examples of how you outwitted the defenders?

(Answer: By a sprint as I was faster than them, using a feint dodge or selling a dummy as they are quicker than me.)

CHAPTER 2

DECISION-TRAINING PRACTICES FOR COACHING BALL SKILLS

Netball is physiologically demanding and players must exercise a high level of skill, performing passing, catching and shooting skills in an ever-changing tactical and pressurized environment. An individual must also be able to make accurate decisions in terms of when, where and why a particular skill needs to be executed. For example, what type of pass will be best to use in this situation? How will you decide when to release the ball? Or what are your passing options?

This chapter will present an overview of the following catching and throwing skills:

* Catching (two-handed and one-handed).
* Chest pass.
* Bounce pass.
* Shoulder pass.
* Overhead pass.

Goal attack reading the cues of the defender marking the goal shooter.

CATCHING

For the static two-handed catch a player must prepare to catch by keeping their eyes on the ball, moving their body to meet the ball and extending the arms to reach towards the ball.

At the execution phase of the catch, the player must have their fingers spread around the back and sides of the ball and they must squeeze onto the ball. The thumbs are in the middle and with the first fingers ensure a 'W' shape behind the ball. The hands and arms 'give' on contact and the ball is brought into the body in preparation to throw.

Key coaching points:
* Eyes on the ball.
* Fingers spread.
* 'W' shape with thumbs and first finger behind the ball.
* 'Give' on contact with the arms and hands.

When catching a ball two-handed on the move a player must also keep their head up and jump to catch in order to control the momentum. A player must land in a balanced position with their weight over the landing foot or both feet. The hips should be lowered and the knees flexed to provide more stability and control to the landing position.

Often a player will catch the ball and turn simultaneously in the air, in order to face the direction of play. This means the player does not need to pivot after landing and therefore has more time to process information and make a decision of who to pass to. For this to be executed correctly a player must drive up and extend towards the ball with feet off the ground, ensuring that the turn begins at the take-off point. To initiate the turn, the player must take off by pushing in the direction of the turn and should move their head, shoulders and hips in the intended direction.

On occasions within the game there is a need to catch one-handed, particularly if the ball is out to the side of the body and at a greater distance away from the body. A player will extend their catching arm and hand towards the ball and as soon as possible they will add the second hand as the ball is brought into the body. A player must also 'give' when catching so as to absorb the impact. The ball is controlled by the fingers being spread around it. A coach should ensure that

Goal attack electing to square the ball on the overlap.

players develop the ability to catch one-handed with both the right and left hand.

THROWING

Any player must develop their throwing skills by developing competence in the full range of throws. A throw is only successful in the game if the ball carrier has made the correct decision and addresses the many perceptual factors.

> **Perceptual Factors**
> * What type of pass to use – is it a short- or long-distance pass?
> * Who does the player pass to, given more than one option?
> * Where does the player pass?
> * What weight of pass to use – a flat, fast pass or lofted in the air?
> * When should the ball be thrown?

For the successful execution of all throws there are some common coaching points that should be stressed to any player. A player should always keep their eyes on the target, keep their body balanced throughout the pass and also follow through with the arms and hands towards the target.

Chest Pass

The chest pass is most commonly used over shorter distances when a defender is not between the ball carrier and receiver. This pass allows the player to send a controlled flat, fast pass that is easily controlled. The pass starts from the two-handed catching position, with the ball being held at chest height. In the preparation phase the fingers must be spread behind the ball, keeping the elbows low and relaxed. In the execution phase the body weight is transferred forwards and the ball is released as the arms and wrists extend. A player must follow through with their hands, fingers and arms.

Effective decision-making is crucial around the shooting circle.

Catching in the air.

Seeking out the best passing option.

Key coaching points:
* Ball is held at chest height.
* Elbows low and relaxed.
* Maintain 'W' shape used when catching.
* Transfer the body weight forwards when throwing.
* Extend the arms and wrists on the follow-through.

Bounce Pass

The two-handed bounce pass is used over short distances and is most commonly employed by players when passing to someone in a confined space, for example a wing attack or centre passing on the circle edge to a shooter inside the shooting circle. This type of pass works effectively against tall defence, who have strength in their ability to intercept and challenge any aerial ball being sent to a shooter. In the preparation phase the ball is held just below chest height and applies a similar action to the chest pass. In the execution phase the ball should bounce two-thirds of the distance between the ball carrier and receiver, with the

bounce often being kept low to prevent a defender intercepting it.

On occasions a one-handed bounce pass is used, which does enable the player to obtain a better angle for the pass and also to protect the ball from a defender. In the preparation phase the ball is taken to the side of the body and kept at waist height. To execute the one-handed pass the player takes a step across with the opposite foot to the throwing arm.

Shoulder Pass

This pass is used over longer distances and requires considerable power. In the preparation phase the ball carrier takes up a balanced starting position with the opposite foot forwards in relation to the throwing arm. The ball is positioned just above the shoulder with fingers spread behind the ball. A young or novice player may use the second hand to steady the ball prior to executing the pass. The ball is positioned behind the shoulder to ensure that maximum power is gained. As the ball is released the hips rotate as the hand, arm and shoulder moves forwards towards the receiver. The body weight is transferred forwards in the direction of the pass and onto the front foot. In the follow-through the arm, hand and fingers extend towards the target.

Key coaching points:
* Ball held above and behind the shoulder.
* Opposite foot forwards to throwing arm.
* As the ball is released the hips rotate.
* On execution the hand, arm and shoulder extend forwards.

Overhead Pass

This pass allows the ball carrier to clear a defender's reach and the overhead pass can be high, floating or straight. The ball is held above the head and the position of the fingers and hands is the same as for the two-handed catch. The ball is taken slightly behind the head with the wrists extended backwards in the preparation phase. As the ball is released the arms extend to propel the ball forwards to the receiver. The power for this throw is from the elbows as the arm extends.

PRACTICE: PASS AND CUT
NUMBERS: EIGHT

**Players work in pairs and must pass the ball within the space, making
sure they move towards the ball carrier.**

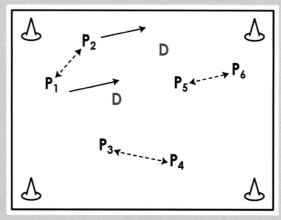

Practice Outcomes

* To move the ball in pairs around the space, moving toward the ball carrier to received using a range of passes.

* To remain ball side in relation to the floating defenders in the space.

* To use a preliminary move away to draw a defender and to open up space to received back side..

* To move into the free space and balance the attacking area..

Task/Group Organization

Use a quarter of the court area, making sure players work up and down (four cones define the area)

Each pair should take on the role of defence (no bibs to overload the attacker in terms of their vision)

Defenders move around between the pairs of attack, trying to get ball side but do not attempt to intercept.

Work for 30 seconds.

Progressions and Differentiation

Defenders can go for the interception or defend the pass (stage 2)

Attacker must move out to a line before receiving or smaller space.

Potential Question to Pose

What might the ball carrier do to outwit a defender?

(Answer: fake the ball to assist the received gaining a ball side position.)

PRACTICE: COLOUR CONE NUMBERS: THREE

Attacking pair must move to the coloured cones and pass the ball in the area while being defended.

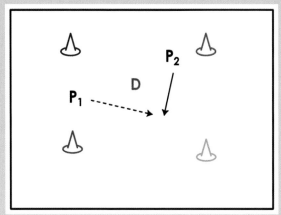

Practice Outcomes

* To pass trhe ball five times in the space while on a 2v1 using a range of passes.

* To receive ball side and penetrate the space (moving up and down).

* To use a fake or preliminary move to outwit the defender.

Task/Group Organization

Half of the third area is used.

The attacking pair must complete five flat passes without the defender being between the ball carrier and receiver.

Attackers complete five passes, repeat three times and change roles.

Progressions and Differentiation

The is could become a 2v2 or 3v1.

Reduce the space for the practice (harder for the attack).

Potential Question to Pose

What can the ball carrier do to decived the defender?

(Answer: fake the pass.)

PRACTICE: CENTRE POINT NUMBERS: SIX TO TWELVE

Individual players work on a double lead in the space, working on their vision.

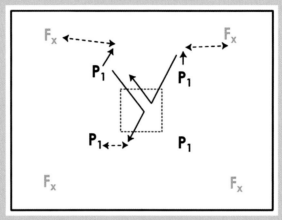

Practice Outcomes

* To perform a double lead before receiving the ball.

* To use peripheral vision to locate the free feeder.

Progressions and Differentiation

Players must use a range of methods to change direction, for example roll, reverse-pivot or feint-dodge.

Task/Group Organization

Four feeders form a square and each have a ball.

A centre point is defined in the practice and each player must move through prior to receiving the ball.

Players pass the ball back to the feeder.

Each player receives eight passes and changes with a feeder.

Players work three repetitions in each role.

Potential Question to Pose

What must the attacker focus upon in the practice?

(Answer: Location of attackers and the free feeder.)

PRACTICE: THREE OFFERS
NUMBERS: NINE

Working from three points of a triangle, attackers offer and re-offer within the defined area.

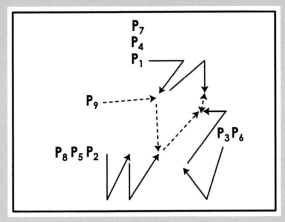

Practice Outcomes

* To ensure there are simultaneous offers for the ball from each attacker, that is, attackers when working in the space never stand still.

* To move the ball flat and fast as there are no defenders to contest.

* To read off the front player(s) and provide at least two passing options for the ball carrier.

* To select the appropriate pass.

Task/Group Organization

Players should position themselves at one of the points.

Three players move from the points, all offering for the ball (Player 9 in the diagram was the last to receive in the previous trio so passes on to the next group).

The first person who received the ball from P9, which is P1 here, must receive the ball after P2 and P3 have received and pass on to the next three moving in.

Progressions and Differentiation

Players must each receive the ball twice before moving out of the area (harder).

One or two defenders can float in the space to intercept.

Potential Question to Pose

What cues will help a player's timing when offering for the ball carrier?

(Answer: Speed of the ball carrier when preparing to throw.)

PRACTICE: COLOUR TRACK NUMBERS: TWO

The players will work on their capacity to process information and move at speed to receive the ball.

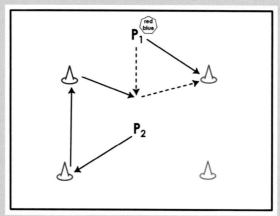

Practice Outcomes

* To use a sprint and change of direction.

* To pass ahead of the receiver within the space.

* To pass the ball flat and fast.

* To focus on the ball at all times.

* To move on to the ball at speed.

* To use a range of passing options.

Task/Group Organization

Four coloured cones are required and players work in half of a third area.

P1 calls two colours and P2 must move to both cones before receiving a pass from P1 in the centre of the space.

P1 must then move to receive a pass at one of the coloured cones not used by P2 (in this example she moves to green).

The practice restarts with P1 at green.

Progressions and Differentiation

P1 and P2 can pass the ball four times, moving to a coloured cone with all cones having been covered after the four passes.

The practice is easier when calling one colour only.

Potential Question to Pose

What must the mover focus upon in the practice and how can she do this?

(Answer: The ball and by angling the upper body when moving away.)

PRACTICE: COLOUR AND NUMBER
NUMBERS: THREE

The players will work on their capacity to process information and move at speed to receive the ball while being defended in the space.

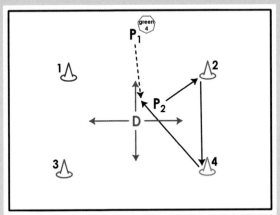

Practice Outcomes

* To maintain the speed of movement while under additional cognitive pressure.

* To execute a change of direction at the cone and accelerate out of this.

* To use a range of movement skills to outwit the defender in the centre space, receiving ball-side.

Task/Group Organization

Four coloured cones are required and players work in a half of a third area.

Each cone has a number, with P1 calling a colour and a number to which P2 moves.

The ball is passed in the centre space where the defender is covering (this should be defined).

After six repetitions P1 and P2 should change roles.

Progressions and Differentiation

Call three colours/numbers, for example 1, blue and 4.

Call only numbers or colours (easier).

Potential Question to Pose

What should be assessed about the defender in this practice?

(Answer: How fast they are, how quickly they change direction and if they are right- or left-side dominant.)

PRACTICE: PASSING INTERCHANGE
NUMBERS: FOUR

The players pass and move in the space and on the call will interchange to work with a player from another pairing.

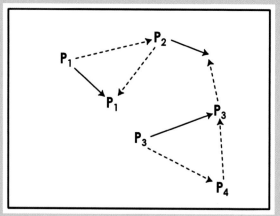

Practice Outcomes

* To use a range of passing techniques while moving at speed within the space.

* To balance the court area with the other pairs working in the space.

* To execute a fast catch and release action.

* To move the ball flat and fast.

Task/Group Organization

Four players working in pairs within a half of a third area.

Players are passing and moving in the space.

On the coach call of 'change' the player not in possession of the ball must switch to work with another partner.

Players should work for 30–40 seconds.

Progressions and Differentiation

Increase the number of pairs in each area to make the switch more complex.

Each pass must be different from the previous one executed.

Potential Question to Pose

What cues must a player attend to?

(Answer: Where other pairs are moving, the speed of release and movement of the player being worked with.)

PRACTICE: QUAD PASS
NUMBERS: FOUR TO TWELVE

The players must pass and move the ball in their group, moving around a cone prior to receiving.

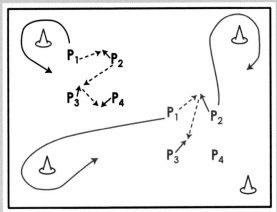

Practice Outcomes

* To use a range of passing techniques while moving at speed within the space.

* To balance the court area with the other pairs working in the space.

* To execute a fast catch and release action (one second release).

* To move the ball flat and fast.

* To pass on the straight line.

Task/Group Organization

One to three groups of four can work in a half of a third area.

Four cones define the area of a different colour.

Players must pass the ball within their group, ensuring they cover all corners of the area.

Players should work for 30–40 seconds.

Move to cone before receiving.

Progressions and Differentiation

Increase the number of pairs in each area or reduce the size of the space.

Each pass must be different from the previous one executed.

Potential Question to Pose

What considerations are there when moving out to a cone?

(Answer: Trying not to move through the line of the ball and moving away from the group passing the ball.)

PRACTICE: REACTION BALL
NUMBERS: FIVE

A player is placed under pressure to pass and receive while using their vision to sight the colour of a card on the periphery of the practice.

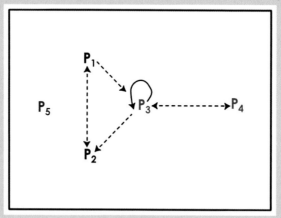

Practice Outcomes

* To read the cues and pass to the free player without a ball.

* To step forwards into the pass.

* To turn in the air quickly after receiving the ball, giving more time to sight the free player.

* To use peripheral vision.

* To use a fast, flat pass.

Task/Group Organization

P1 and P2 are passing a ball.

P4 on the command 'pass' distributes a lofted pass to P3, who turns to face P1 and P2.

P3 must pass to the free player (P2) and at the same time call the colour of the card held by P5.

P3 receives a pass from P1 and passes to P4.

Players should complete eight repetitions.

Progressions and Differentiation

P5 holds up another colour for P3 to call out when receiving the pass from P1 or P2.

P5 moves further away or to the non-dominant side of P3.

Potential Question to Pose

How can P3 prepare for the release to P1 or P2?

(Answer: By seeing P1 and P2 early when turning in the air, while keeping the body upright and looking ahead to aid vision.)

PRACTICE: LEADS
NUMBERS: FOUR

Players must execute a range of double leads to receive the ball and must pass the ball to the space ahead of the receiver.

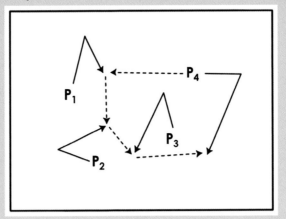

Practice Outcomes

* To use a range of double leads to receive the ball.

* The ball carrier should turn fully to the group of players and select the correct passing option.

* To know when to pass in relation to the direction and depth of the receiver's movement.

* To pass on the straight line or use the overlap player.

Progressions and Differentiation

The three moves must offer a short, mid and long lead.

Vary the speed of the pass and use the aerial ball for a player to receive in the air.

Task/Group Organization

P1 to P4 execute a variety of double leads and must not repeat the same lead carried out immediately before.

There should be twelve passes before a 30-second rest/recovery period (×4).

Players should work in a half of a third area.

Potential Question to Pose

What affects the timing of the ball carrier's release?

(Answer: The speed of the receiver's movement.)

PRACTICE: ON GUARD
NUMBERS: EIGHT

Players must pass the ball in the group of four while being mindful of the defenders positioned on the outer perimeter of the practice.

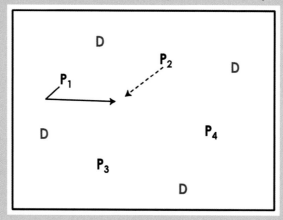

Practice Outcomes

* To use a fast, flat pass.

* To use one's vision to sight the defender(s) who are off-line.

* To select the passing option on the straight line and ball-side of a defender.

* The ball carrier to turn fully to the group of players.

* To know when to pass in relation to the direction and depth of the receiver's movement.

* To pass on the straight line or use the overlap player.

Progressions and Differentiation

Defence can defend by using one on one, zoning the space, or mix-up.

Defence has one attempt to 'fly' for the intercept and must return to the perimeter.

Task/Group Organization

P1 to P4 move the ball between themselves, moving up and down and penetrating the available space.

There should be twelve passes before a 30-second rest/recovery period (×4).

Players should work in a half of a third area.

Defenders should interchange with the attack after two repetitions.

Defence initially retrieve any loose ball.

Potential Question to Pose

How might another attacker help to protect the receiver's space?

(Answer: Attackers might screen to create a free space and undefended situation for another player to receive.)

PRACTICE: NEGOTIATE NUMBERS: FOUR

Two attacking players within a space are moving to the cones and receiving from the static passers.

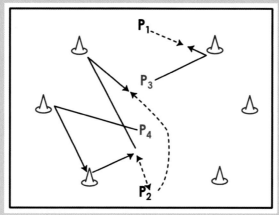

Practice Outcomes

* To read the attacker's movement and know when this is a lead to receive.

* To know when to pass in relation to the direction and depth of the receiver's movement.

* To execute a pass for the attacker to move on to in the space.

* To negotiate another player in the space when passing and moving.

Task/Group Organization

P3 and P4 are moving to the cones and will vary the intensity of the movement.

On a sprint, the player will receive the pass from one of the static passers, P1 or P2.

P3 or 4 give the ball back to the static passer they received from and continue.

Six to eight repetitions and then change roles.

Progressions and Differentiation

P3 or P4 pass to the other static passer, or must read off each other and move to opposite cones to balance space.

Potential Question to Pose

When should the player release the ball?

(Answer: When the attacker has changed direction at the cone and sights the ball.)

PRACTICE: NUMBER CHANGE
NUMBERS: TWELVE

Players pass within the space and will interchange individually to become a member of another group.

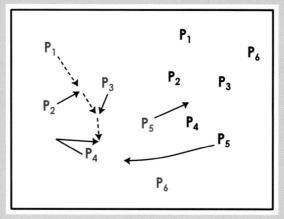

Practice Outcomes

* To pass the ball at speed within the group.

* To pass the ball on a 1-, 2- and 3-second release.

* To use the aerial ball (lob or shoulder pass) for players moving into a back space to receive.

Task/Group Organization

P1–6 move the ball around in their group.

A number is called out by either the coach or a leading player (number 5 is called in this example).

Player 5 moves to join the opposite group and must receive the ball on entry into this new passing group.

Work for 30–45 seconds and rest.

Progressions and Differentiation

The coach can call two numbers to interchange.

The second number called could stay in their own group but be a defender.

Potential Question to Pose

How can players in the group help P5 to locate the space to receive?

(Answer: By clearing to create space.)

PRACTICE: TWO BALL SQUARE
NUMBERS: SIX

An attacker is receiving the ball from a player after moving to a cone and must send the ball to a free player who is static on the perimeter.

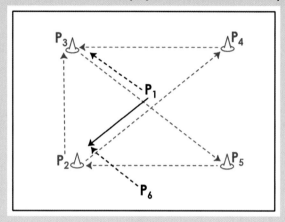

Practice Outcomes

* To pass the ball flat and fast at speed.

* To pass the ball on a 1-second release.

* To use peripheral vision to sight a free player to whom to pass.

* To pass the ball ahead of the moving player.

Task/Group Organization

P2–5 are static and passing the ball between themselves.

P1 moves to a cone and receives a pass from P6.

P1 must pass the ball to P2 or P5 who is not in possession of the other ball or about to receive a pass.

The player who received the pass from P1 sends it back to P6 to then repeat.

Work for 30–45 seconds and rest.

Progressions and Differentiation

P1 moves to two cones before receiving a pass, or must receive at each cone.

P2–5 may put in a loose ball that must be retrieved and passed back by P1.

Potential Question to Pose

What makes an effective catch and release on 1 second?

(Answer: Giving with the elbows when catching will be the preparation to release.)

PRACTICE: PASSING CIRCLE
NUMBERS: SIX TO EIGHT

The ball is passed around the circle, but cannot be given to the player either side of the ball carrier and two defenders can go for a flying intercept.

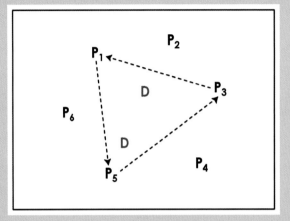

Practice Outcomes

* To select the correct pass to give in relation to the position of the defence.

* To vary the weight and trajectory of the pass in relation to the defender position.

* To use peripheral vision to locate the position of the defender(s).

* To release the ball as quickly as possible in 1 or 2 seconds.

Task/Group Organization

P1–6 are static and passing the ball but cannot pass to a player immediately next to them in the circle.

The two defenders have one attempt on each pass to try for a flying intercept.

Defence should rotate with the circle players after fifteen passes.

Progressions and Differentiation

On every fourth catch the player who received the pass must change with the person who sent it, for example if P6 was the passer and P2 the receiver they would switch places in the circle.

Potential Question to Pose

What cues should P1–6 read?

(Answer: Defender's feet and the direction they face will indicate where they are likely to move.)

PRACTICE: HIGH BALL
NUMBERS: FOUR

Players pass a high lofted ball to each other for the receiver to elevate on to and catch with one hand.

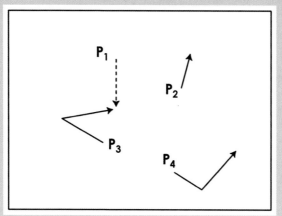

Practice Outcomes

* To use a one-handed catch when receiving a high ball.

* To use the second hand on the ball as early as possible after the catch.

* To execute a pass into the air at the correct height above the receiver.

* To pass a high ball to a moving player.

* To select the preferred passing option from three offers (on the straight line).

Progressions and Differentiation

Use a two-handed catch (easier).

Add a defender.

Use a range of passing options.

Task/Group Organization

P1–4 pass the ball within a space (three to four groups per third area).

Players must initially lead away from the ball carrier and receive a high ball on the second lead.

All three players offer for the ball and the ball carrier selects one to pass to.

Potential Question to Pose

For a high ball to be effective where should this be placed?

(Answer: Above the receiver, away from the defender side and players should know each other's range when elevating.)

PRACTICE: FAKE AND PASS
NUMBERS: SIX

Players receive a pass on the move and must deceive the defender.

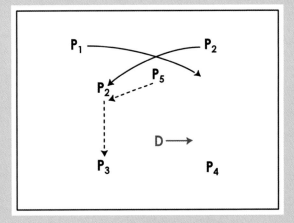

Practice Outcomes

* To catch the ball effectively on the move and deliver a pass to a static receiver.

* To use a fake of the pass to outwit the defender.

* To select the best passing option.

Progressions and Differentiation

Defender does not have to move by the 2-second count (harder for the attacker).

Players can move to receive if the fake does not commit the defender.

Task/Group Organization

P1 and P2 lead by crossing over sides and P5 sends the ball to either player.

P2 receives the ball in the diagram and must fake the pass to move the defender.

The defender must move in one direction after 2 seconds.

The practice can run from the other end with P3 and 4 moving and D as passer.

Work for 1 minute.

Potential Question to Pose

What makes a good fake pass?

(Answer: Ball carrier using the eyes or body positioning to deceive, or the fake must be carried out assertively.)

PRACTICE: FREE PLAYER
NUMBERS: SIX

Players passing and moving in the space and must ensure that the ball goes to a free player.

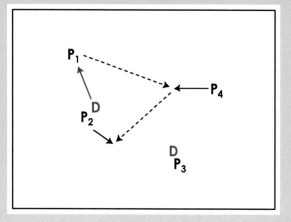

Practice Outcomes

* To catch the ball effectively on the move and pass to another player free from a defender.

* To use a range of passing options.

* To pass to ball-side.

* To avoid passing over two defenders.

Task/Group Organization

P1–4 pass and move in the space and must not pass to a player who is marked.

Defenders must change the player they are marking after each pass.

After twelve passes the defence must change roles.

Progressions and Differentiation

Reduce the space (harder for the attack).

Remove one defender (easier).

Potential Question to Pose

What are the strengths of the two defenders a player was up against?

(Answer: Faster, good on the left side when marking, or drops their head when changing direction.)

PRACTICE: TWO BALL SQUARE
NUMBERS: EIGHT TO TEN

Players must receive the ball from the right and pass ahead while being defended in the centre of the space.

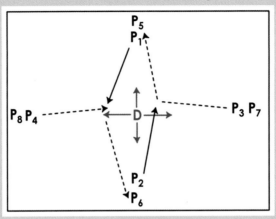

Practice Outcomes

* To catch the ball effectively on the move and pass ahead while negotiating a defender.

* To pass the ball ahead of the receiver and to ball-side.

* To use a fast, flat pass.

Task/Group Organization

P1 receives from P4 and P2 from P3 and passes the ball ahead to the opposite line (they also join the opposite line).

The defender must remain in the centre space and try to intercept one of the passes coming to the mover.

After 30 seconds the defender should be changed.

Work for 1 minute, then rest.

Progressions and Differentiation

Add another defender in the centre.

Receive from the left side.

Players receiving at the line could execute a lead for the ball.

Potential Question to Pose

What are the benefits of moving up close on the defender?

(Answer: Can then step across them and stop their move to the ball.)

PRACTICE: ATTACKING ZONES
NUMBERS: FIVE TO SEVEN

Three attacking players must move into a zone to receive while moving to the circle edge to feed the circle for a shooting opportunity.

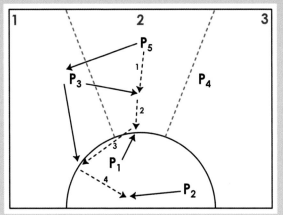

Practice Outcomes

* To pass the ball effectively while working to the circle edge.

* To balance the court by not being in the same zone as the other attacker.

* To move into a zone to receive the ball.

* To pass on the straight line wherever possible.

Task/Group Organization

Four zones are defined with spot markers, if necessary (the shooting circle is also a zone).

A player must move into another zone to receive the ball.

P5 passes to P3, moving to the centre zone; P3 passes to P1 on the straight line. P1 passes to P3 on the edge, who passes to P2 for a shooting opportunity.

Progressions and Differentiation

Add a defender in each zone (harder).

Potential Question to Pose

When should a player move to receive a pass?

(Answer: When the ball carrier is balanced and looking to pass the ball.)

PRACTICE: SIX PASS
NUMBERS: FIVE

This practice involves passing the ball to a static and moving player while at times being defended in the space.

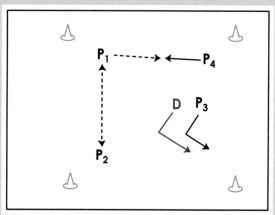

Practice Outcomes

* To pass the ball effectively while in a 2v1 situation.

* To execute a pass on the ball-side of the defender.

* To use the fake to outwit the defender.

Task/Group Organization

Four cones define the area.

P1 and P2 pass the ball six times before sighting and passing the ball to the unmarked player.

P3 and P4 must then pass the ball six times while in a 2v1 situation.

P1 and P2 can be used to offload the ball on no more than two occasions.

Two reps and then rest, but all players should change roles.

Progressions and Differentiation

Add another defender on P1 and P2.

P3 and P4 must pass the ball over a line after the six passes to score.

Easier option: pass four times only.

Potential Question to Pose

How can two attacking players create difficulties for the defender?

(Answer: Create width between attackers, use a change of direction or use a front cut.)

PRACTICE: PASSING MAZE
NUMBERS: FOUR

The practice involves a player collecting a loose ball and passing on to a free player.

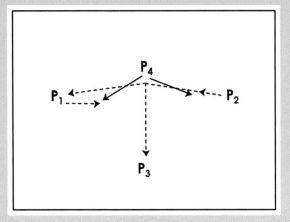

Practice Outcomes

* To retrieve the loose ball effectively using a two- or one-handed catch.

* To deliver the ball on the first second back to the free player.

* To pass the ball flat and fast at all times.

Task/Group Organization

Two balls in the practice and P1 and P2 are in possession above.

P4 is the worker and must move to receive a loose ball and pass to the free player, which is P3.

P2 will then release the ball into a space for P4 to move on to and pass to P1; P4 cannot pass to the person who released the ball.

Six to eight reps, then change the worker.

Progressions and Differentiation

Add a defender on P4 (harder).

Have one ball only (easier).

P1–3 move to receive the pass from P4 (harder).

Potential Question to Pose

What is important about P4's body angle when working?

(Answer: Should be able to see all players and if moving away angle the upper body to sight the players.)

PRACTICE: TENNIS BALL NUMBERS: TWO

Players have a tennis ball and must retrieve the ball after only one bounce, working their hand–eye coordination for catching.

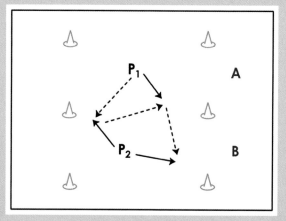

Practice Outcomes

* To move at speed to collect the tennis ball after no more than one bounce.

* To try to outwit the opponent using a fake or the eyes to deceive.

* To locate and pass effectively to the free space in the opponent's half of the area.

Task/Group Organization

Two zones are marked out using six cones.

Players use an underarm throw and the ball must be released in an upwards motion when aiming for a space in the opponent's half.

A point is scored if the opponent does not receive the ball after one bounce, or if the ball is thrown out of the area.

Progressions and Differentiation

Smaller area is harder for the players to throw into a space.

Play a 2v2.

Use a netball and a range of passes.

Potential Question to Pose

Why is the speed of release important in this practice?

(Answer: The defender may be repositioning and has less time to react on a fast release.)

PRACTICE: ON GUARD
NUMBERS: FOUR

Two players must defend an area and move at speed to catch the ball.

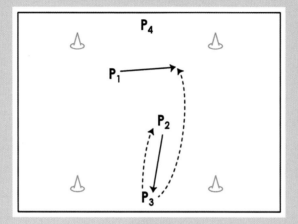

Practice Outcomes

* To use effective catching techniques when two balls are randomly thrown into the area.

* To communicate with the other player to ensure the ball is caught by the nearest player.

* To use a fast, flat pass.

Progressions and Differentiation

Both balls are sent in simultaneously (harder).

P3 and P4 place the ball into the practice sequentially (easier).

Task/Group Organization

P1 and P2 are the workers and P3 and P4 both have a ball.

P3 and P4 randomly throw in the netballs and they must be caught after no more than one bounce.

Once caught the ball must be passed to either P3 or P4.

P1 and P2 score a point after five successful catches are made.

Work for 30 seconds and change roles.

Potential Question to Pose

How should P1 and P2 position to catch the ball?

(Answer: Take front and back or cover a side each.)

PRACTICE: WALL OF COLOUR I
NUMBERS: FOUR

**Two players pass and move in the space, receiving the ball in all areas
and testing passing accuracy by aiming for the colour called out.**

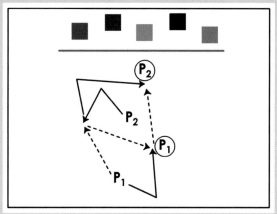

Practice Outcomes

* To pass ahead of the moving player.

* To extend the arms to catch on the move.

* To execute an accurate pass.

Task/Group Organization

Five pieces of card are stuck on the wall.

P1 and P2 move the ball in the space using a double lead.

The area of work should be defined using spot markers if necessary.

The coach or a static player in the group will call a colour and the player in possession must aim to hit the marker on the wall from their location.

Repeat four times, then rest.

Progressions and Differentiation

The call is made when the player is furthest away from the wall (harder).

The player can use a give and go with the other player to get nearer the wall before aiming for the colour (easier).

Potential Question to Pose

What part of the body is important for accuracy in passing?

(Answer: Focus on the target, step to the target when passing and follow through in the direction of the target.)

PRACTICE: WALL OF COLOUR 2
NUMBERS: FOUR

**Four players pass and move in the space receiving the ball in all areas
and test passing accuracy by aiming for the colour called out.**

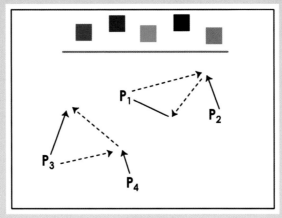

Practice Outcomes

* To pass ahead of the moving player.

* To extend the arms to catch on the move.

* To execute an accurate pass to the free colour.

Task/Group Organization

Five pieces of card are stuck on the wall.

Pairs move the ball in the space using a double lead.

The area of work should be defined using spot markers if necessary.

The coach or a player static in the group will call two colours and the nearest player to the wall selects one of the colour targets and the second player must hit the other colour called.

Progressions and Differentiation

The second pass can go to the same colour if on the straight line.

A defender could be floating in the space and mark the pass to the wall (harder).

Potential Question to Pose

When being marked (stage two) what can the ball carrier do to help sight the colour?

(Answer: Step back, to the side or around the stage two defender.)

PRACTICE: WALL OF COLOUR 3
NUMBERS: FOUR

Pass and move in the space, receiving the ball in all areas and test passing accuracy by aiming for the coloured markers on the wall.

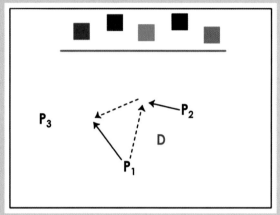

Practice Outcomes

* To pass ahead of the moving player.

* To extend the arms to catch on the move.

* To execute an accurate pass to the colour markers.

* To pass without the defender being between the ball carrier and receiver.

* To pass the ball accurately to all colour markers on the wall, not hitting any colour twice (five points for each hit).

Task/Group Organization

Five pieces of card are stuck on the wall.

Pairs move the ball in a defined space, complete four passes, then aim for a marker.

P3 checks the number of passes and marker accuracy and will change with either P1 or P2 after each rotation.

P1 and P2 must remember which marker has been hit or aimed at and repeat until all five have been attempted.

Progressions and Differentiation

P3 can be used if the defender is between P1 and P2, but this does not count as one of the five passes.

Potential Question to Pose

If close to the wall what pass should be used?

(Answer: Chest pass.)

PRACTICE: NUMBER LINE
NUMBERS: SIX

Players must pass the ball in a set sequence, while offering and re-offering in the space.

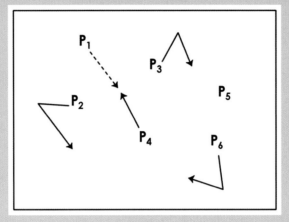

Practice Outcomes

* To pass ahead of the moving player.

* To extend the arms to catch on the move.

* To execute single and double leads in the practice.

* To balance the space and move into free space to receive.

Task/Group Organization

Six passes equals a goal.

Players are numbered from 1–6 and cannot pass to the number before or after them, for example player 1 cannot pass to 6 or 2.

The number of passes made before an error is counted in 30 seconds.

A team of six are resting and counting the success of the other team and then change over – repeat four times for each team.

Progressions and Differentiation

Add defender(s).

Players must move to a cone after they have passed the ball.

Throw with the non-dominant hand.

Potential Question to Pose

If P1 has the ball how can P6 and P2 help the decision-making of P1?

(Answer: Lead away, indicating they should not be used.)

PRACTICE: SPACE SHUFFLE
NUMBERS: SIX

This practice works on the accuracy of the pass to space while contending with static defence.

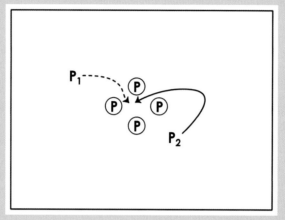

Practice Outcomes

* To pass ahead of the moving player.

* To extend the arms to catch on the move.

* To pass the ball away from the defender's reach.

* To sight the moving player early as the ball carrier.

Task/Group Organization

P1 faces away from the five players and tosses the ball high, turns in the air and looks to pass to a moving player.

Players decide who will move in each of the six repetitions and in this example it is P2.

P1 must pass the ball as P2 moves within and between the other four players.

P2 will pass back to P1.

Static players can reach up to intercept.

Progressions and Differentiation

P2 then passes back to P1 and they attempt four passes while the other players defend the space (not one on one).

All players can receive a pass once P2 has received the pass from P1.

Potential Question to Pose

How can P2 ensure the pass is received successfully?

(Answer: Could reach out to the side to receive or reach forward away from the static players.)

PRACTICE: NAME GAME
NUMBERS: FOUR

This practice works on the information-processing capacity of the ball carrier and effective passing and catching.

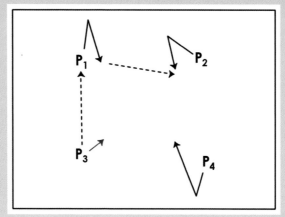

Practice Outcomes

* To use effective catching technique by extending the arms to receive.

* To pass ahead of the moving player.

* To pass the ball ahead of the receiver.

* To be able to see two or more players as the ball carrier.

Task/Group Organization

P1–4 must pass the ball in the defined area (half of a third) and there must be three offers for the ball carrier each time.

P3 has the ball here and must call the name of a player that they believe is not the best passing option.

P3 will then pass to another player who repeats.

Work for 30–45 seconds and rest.

Progressions and Differentiation

Players must call the name of the front mover and pass to another option.

Add a floating defender (harder).

Potential Question to Pose

What makes a good passing option?

(Answer: Decisive movement on the straight line.)

CHAPTER 3

DECISION-TRAINING PRACTICES FOR COACHING ATTACKING SKILLS

The methods utilized to get free draw upon several movement skills outlined in Chapter 1. A player must be able to get free from a stationary and moving position within the game using their vision and powers of decision-making to identify a suitable front or back space into which to move. The experienced performer will be autonomous in their execution of the skills and would be able to demonstrate the ability to vary the attacking skills used according to the tactical and technical strengths and weaknesses of the opposition. In game conditions a player must also be able to read the necessary cues around them, work to get free under pressure and ultimately execute a well-timed move into the available free space.

It is vital that a coach offers practices that work to enhance a player's decision-making powers and this can be achieved by adding the perceptual factors into the training programme.

The centre must sight all options at the centre pass.

> **The Perceptual Factors**
> * Space: Where should a player move to?
> * Timing: When should a player move and at what point should they break free?
> * Pace: At what speed should they change to break free?
> * Direction: Should the player move straight or diagonal? Forwards or backwards?

The attacking skills can often incorporate one or more of the following movement skills: sprinting and changes of pace and direction. The sprint to receive the ball is commonly referred to as a 'lead'. Some of the most important methods used to get free are outlined below:

* Straight and diagonal lead.
* Double lead.
* Dodge and double-dodge.
* Protecting a space.

Straight and Diagonal Lead

The correct sprinting technique is applied to this attacking move and the player must focus ahead on the

Athleticism and vision are key to success.

ball and the available space. The initial take-off is important and the attacker must use a high knee lift to gain momentum to move away from the defender. The direction of the lead is dependent upon the position of the defender(s) and should the defence mark from a side position, the player will often execute a diagonal move. Often defence will mark from the in-front position and a player may then decide to lead to the back space (either diagonally or straight).

A player must practise the diagonal lead from both sides and in a forwards and backwards direction. It is also important to practise this lead by taking off on the inside and outside foot. The outside foot take-off allows the attacker to drive out quickly on the diagonal and away from the defender. The inside foot take-off allows the attacker to cut off the movement path of the defender.

Double Lead

A double lead is executed if on the first lead the ball has not been received. A double lead often combines the attacking sprint with a change of direction and can be used to commit a defender in one direction before moving into a free space. This lead requires a convincing body movement and is often effective when the defender is persistent and marking tightly one on one. The change of direction after the first lead, if executed quickly, ultimately leaves the defender out of position and opens up a space in which to receive the pass.

The various combinations open up the forwards or back space for the attacker and the up and back lead combination is useful when the defender has maintained a strong defensive position as the attacker has moved up the court. This move can also open up space when there is a potentially crowded situation. The change of direction at the end of the first lead must be implemented when the ball carrier is ready to release the ball. If moving backwards the attacker must maintain their vision on the ball in order to monitor the flight and time the jump to receive.

When using a double lead to get free a player may use the reverse pivot to change direction and this is effective when a defender is marking closely in the front position. The reverse pivot involves the attacker turning out and away from the defender marking them.

Key coaching points for the reverse pivot:
* On the balls of the feet.
* Step to the right using the left leg across the body (moving to the right).

* Reverse the feet for pivoting in the opposite direction.
* Pivot on the right foot.
* Turn the head and shoulders quickly.
* Regain focus quickly on the new direction of movement.

Dodge and Double-Dodge

The dodge can be used to free an opponent and is often executed when the defender is marking very tightly one on one and often from an in-front position. The dodge demands that the attacker executes a feint movement in one direction, often stated as 'selling a dummy to the defender' before moving in another direction. This method is frequently used by players to get free from a stationary position and demands a balanced body position. The attacker feints a movement to one side by planting the foot and using an upper body movement by the leading shoulder before moving off in the other direction. The feint must be strong and convincing, but without the attacker shifting all of the body weight in the direction of this first move.

A powerful turn of the hips will initiate a fast movement into another direction to find a free space.

A double-dodge can be executed which involves two feint movements to commit the defender. This is useful when the attacker has not deceived the defender on the first feint and may need to use another feint to free themselves from the opponent.

Protecting a Space

There are instances in the game where an attacker may wish to protect a space to receive the ball rather than execute a lead or dodge. This is most commonly seen within the goal circle where a shooter works to hold the position by making slight adjustments with the feet to ensure they keep the defender away from the space. The attacker must maintain a strong body position, with knees flexed and a base slightly wider than shoulder-width to maintain stability.

Timing of the move to receive is critical in this skill and the ball carrier will have released the ball before the attacker makes the move. The attacker will hold the position up close to the defender until the last possible

Reading the game and seeing the options.

moment and then lunge, jump or reach to receive the ball, keeping themselves between the ball and defender. The pass must be accurate and consideration should be given to the strengths of the defender in order to decide which pass is the most effective. A defender who has good elevation and intercepts well in the air would be restricted by a bounce pass being placed into the space.

While in possession any team must work to provide at least two forwards and one square option. Attackers will apply the relevant method of getting free following the evaluation of their opponent's strengths and the space available. The attacking move executed can split the defenders and free up space for a fellow teammate to receive the ball. This does mean there could be up to three players moving and attempting to get free and these players must have good vision to ensure that they offer for the ball in a different space. Communication and teamwork are therefore essential between players and the SPACE principles listed here will support a player in using their attacking skills to best effect in a game.

SPACE Top Tips
* **S**can the area for important cues.
* **P**layer at the front initiates.
* **A**lert to all players' intentions.
* **C**learing space for teammates and maintaining court balance.
* **E**xecution of the pass and a well-timed movement.

PRACTICE: PASS AND CLEAR
NUMBERS: THREES

A pass and clear practice sometimes called a three-man weave.

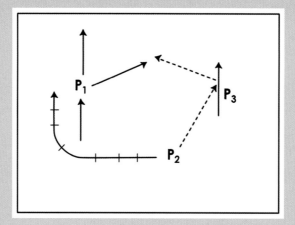

Practice Outcomes

* To use a single lead at speed to receive the ball.

* To move towards the ball carrier to receive.

* To balance the court through the three channels.

* To move the ball through the court, passing ahead of the moving player.

Progressions and Differentiation

Defenders can be positioned to cover the space.

Task/Group Organization

Use a quarter of the court from the goal line to half way.

Three groups should be allocated to work up and down in the space.

Players should work the ball up the court and then return, allowing groups to work in either direction.

Work for one repetition.

Create a 3v1 situation with a defender on a one on one defence.

Potential Question to Pose

Why is it important to fill the free channel?

(Answer: To achieve good court balance.)

PRACTICE: VARIED ATTACK
NUMBERS: SIX TO TWELVE

Players set up three points and must offer and re-offer, using a variety of attacking moves.

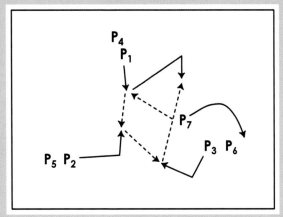

Practice Outcomes

* To use a range of methods to get free, for example roll, feint, reverse pivot, change of pace and so on.

* To move towards the ball carrier to receive.

* To create space for others by using clearing runs.

* To move the ball through the court, passing ahead of the moving player.

Progressions and Differentiation

Defenders can be positioned to cover the space.

A defender can be positioned at the lines to apply pressure.

Task/Group Organization

Use a third area.

Three points are set in a triangle shape.

Players at the front of each line all offer at the same time and continue to do so until all have received the ball.

The player who received first must receive the ball again (P1 in the diagram).

Players cannot perform the same attacking move as the player before them.

Potential Question to Pose

What attacking skill requires more practice by yourself and why?

(Answer: Players should highlight a skill and describe their performance.)

PRACTICE: PRESSURE POINT NUMBERS: FIVES

Players set up three points and the attacker must work to get free from a one on one mark, passing to the free post.

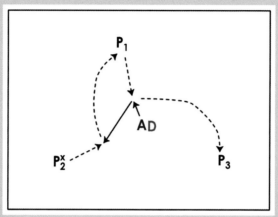

Practice Outcomes

* To receive ball-side and in the front space.

* To close off the defender from the front space.

* To use peripheral vision to sight the free post player while receiving the ball.

* To turn in the air and sight the two post players.

Task/Group Organization

Work in a half of a third area.

Two post players have a ball.

The attacker must move to receive and offload to the free post (not passing back to where the ball was received).

No overhead passes permitted.

Work for six to eight passes and the workers rotate with the posts.

Progressions and Differentiation

Attacker must release the ball on the first second to speed up reactions.

Two floating defence players can apply pressure to a more able player.

Potential Question to Pose

What methods can be used to remain ball-side?

(Answer: Move ahead of the defender and step across their path.)

PRACTICE: LINE TOUCH
NUMBERS: FIVE TO SIX

Three attacking players must receive the ball in the space and show clearing moves to the outside of the area to open up the space.

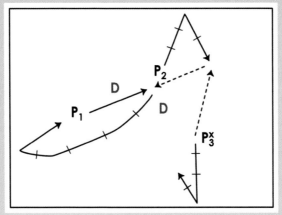

Practice Outcomes

* To receive ball-side and on the straight line.

* To close off the defender from the front space.

* To use clearing moves to open up the space for other attackers.

* To time the move into the space by reading the cues from the ball carrier.

Task/Group Organization

Work in a half of a third area.

3v2 situation (four markers can be used to define the space).

Attackers must receive the ball and then move to touch a line prior to re-offering.

Defenders in the space.

Four uninterrupted passes = 1 point.

Work for 30–40 seconds.

Progressions and Differentiation

Defence can mark one on one (3v3).

Move the ball into the shooting circle after three passes for a shooting opportunity.

Potential Question to Pose

What cues should you read after touching the line?

(Answer: Free space available and read off the front player.)

PRACTICE: CONE SCORER
NUMBERS: SIX

Three attacking players must move towards a marker to score points whilst defended in the space.

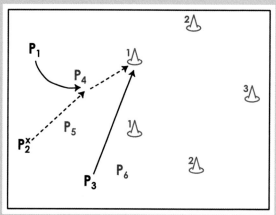

Practice Outcomes

* To use a range of methods to get free from the defence.

* To read off the front player in the attack.

* To devise strategies to outwit the defence and open up point-scoring opportunities.

Task/Group Organization

Work in a half of a third area.

Five cones, each having a points score attached to them between one and three.

Work for 30-40 seconds, aiming to score ten points.

Defence cannot mark or remain static at a cone and must be one on one marking with an attacking player.

Progressions and Differentiation

Reduce the defence to two.

Add more cones.

Add a post for the three-point marker and a shot at goal can be added.

Potential Question to Pose

What strategy could the attack use to outwit the defence?

(Answer: One player may lead to one cone and a second offers to another.)

PRACTICE: PRESSURE FOURS
NUMBERS: TEN TO TWELVE

A 4v4 pressure situation where attackers must complete a run of six passes with an opportunity to use the post players in order to keep possession.

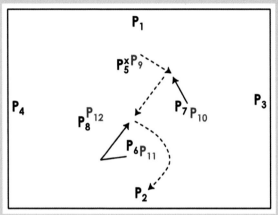

Practice Outcomes

*   To use a range of methods to get free from the defence.

*   To read off the front player in the attack.

*   To devise strategies to outwit the defence and open up point-scoring opportunities.

*   To use a double play if the space ahead is free.

Task/Group Organization

Work in a third area.

Four post players, four attack and four defenders.

Attack must complete six passes to score a point.

Post players can be used to offload the ball, but the pass cannot count as one of the six.

If the defence gains possession, they become the attack.

Progressions and Differentiation

Reduce the number of defenders (easier).

Restrict the use of post players in a run of six passes to one or two (harder).

Reduce the post players to two (harder).

Potential Question to Pose

What might the ball carrier do if a post player is used?

(Answer: A double play may offer time for others to get free.)

PRACTICE: CORNER PRESSURE
NUMBERS: TEN TO FOURTEEN

Attackers must lead for the ball and get free while three corners have defenders who employ different strategies to pressure the player.

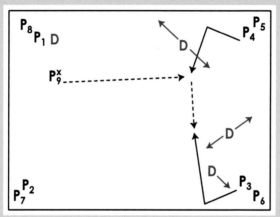

Practice Outcomes

* To use a range of methods to get free from the defence.

* To make the correct decision of who to offload the ball to.

* To assess the strengths of the defence at the corner.

* To identify personal strengths against the different methods of defence.

Progressions and Differentiation

Reduce or add more defenders.

Make the space smaller.

Task/Group Organization

Work in a third area and at four corners.

Ball moves clockwise, but a player can use another corner if a player cannot get free.

Players move onto the next corner after offloading the pass.

Three corners have defence: one on one, defender is sidestepping and a 2v1.

Aim to maintain possession for eight passes and rotate the defence.

Potential Question to Pose

What should be assessed in the defender?

(Answer: Their preferred side, speed and ability to change direction.)

PRACTICE: DRIP-FEED DEFENCE
NUMBERS: EIGHT

Attackers must pass the ball as the defence gradually increases in number against them in the space.

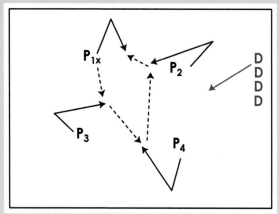

Practice Outcomes

*   To use a range of methods to get free from the defence.

*   To make the correct decision of who to offload the ball to.

*   To pass ball-side of the defence.

*   To use clearing moves to open up the space for others.

*   To ensure there are two offers for the ball carrier.

Task/Group Organization

Work in half of a third area.

Attack must pass the ball without defence for four passes and then one defender moves in after each set of four passes.

The attacking players aim to complete five sets of four passes, with the last set against a 4v4.

The attacking team is allowed one chance at each stage (4v1, 4v2, and so on).

Potential Question to Pose

What should the attack do on a 4v4?

(Answer: Use the width to split the defence and make at least two offers.)

Progressions and Differentiation

Players must touch a line before they can receive a pass.

Start the practice in a 4v2.

PRACTICE: TWO OFFERS
NUMBERS: FOUR

The ball carrier has two options and must select the free player, whilst the ball moves through the court on the straight line or overlap.

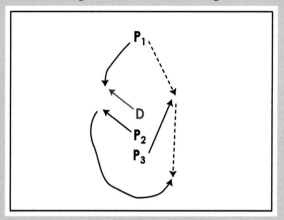

Practice Outcomes

* To read off the front player when offering for the ball.

* To select the best passing option.

* To know when to use the overlap player.

* To pass on the straight line.

Progressions and Differentiation

After the two passes, create a 2v2 situation for six passes.

Add another defender throughout the practice.

Task/Group Organization

Work in a half of a third area.

P1 has the ball and offloads to the free player (P3 here).

P3 can either pass on the straight line to P2 who has cleared and re-offered, or use P1 on the overlap for a square ball.

P2 is the last to receive and the practice runs again in the other direction from this point.

Work for 30 seconds and rest.

Potential Question to Pose

When should the overlap be used here?

(Answer: When the receiver moves too soon or too late.)

PRACTICE: FOUR SPACES
NUMBERS: SIX TO EIGHT

Attacking players must pass the ball and move to another space to receive, while negotiating the defence in each area.

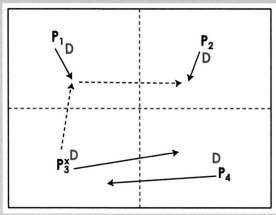

Practice Outcomes

* To select the best passing option.

* To receive the ball in the space on a 1v1.

* To move into a free space.

* To communicate with other players and read off the front mover.

Task/Group Organization

Work in a half of a third area with four divided areas.

Attacking players aim to receive the ball in each area twice to complete a repetition.

Attacking players must pass and then move to a new space.

Only one attacker per space.

Defence must remain in one space.

Progressions and Differentiation

Defence can move freely between spaces.

Add a player to the middle who can be used if others are not free (easier).

Reduce the number of players to 6 (3v3).

Potential Question to Pose

What must the attacker do in the space to outwit the defender?

(Answer: Move the defender and use changes of direction or strong holds.)

PRACTICE: SPACE BALL
NUMBERS: FOURS

The attacking player is marked by a defender and must receive a pass in each area.

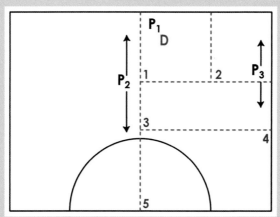

Practice Outcomes

* To use a range of attacking moves to get free on a one on one mark.

* To assess the strengths and areas to exploit in the defender.

* To use a fast take-off step to get free from the one on one defence.

Task/Group Organization

Work in a quarter of the court and identify five spaces as above.

P2 and P3 can be used as many times as required by P1 to ensure the ball is received in each of the five areas.

P2 and P3 can pass to each other to avoid breaking the 3-second rule.

Progressions and Differentiation

Reduce the number of areas to three or four, or allow a player to miss one area (easier).

Add a shot at goal in area 5.

Potential Question to Pose

What might P1 do to outwit a defender?

(Answer: Use a fake or step around the defender.)

PRACTICE: THE GAUNTLET
NUMBERS: SIX

Attacking pairs must pass the ball through each area to the goal line.

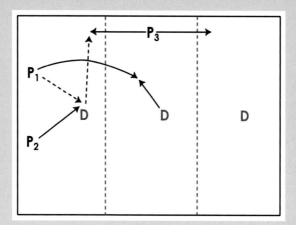

Practice Outcomes

* To receive the pass on ball-side.

* To make the correct passing decision when in possession.

Task/Group Organization

Work in a quarter of the court and identify three spaces as above.

Defence must remain in one area.

P3 can be used on two occasions if the receiver cannot get free.

Both (P1 and P2) players must receive the ball in each area.

Progressions and Differentiation

A defender may move into the next area for a 2v2 situation.

If P3 is used, the passer must interchange (above this would be P2).

Potential Question to Pose

What skills could the attacker use when the defender is facing and ahead of them?

(Answer: Front cut.)

PRACTICE: PASS AND TOUCH
NUMBERS: EIGHT

**Attacking players must pass the ball through the court, clearing the
space by touching a line when the ball is with a feeder.**

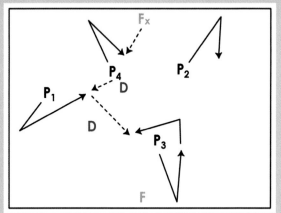

Practice Outcomes

* To receive the pass on the ball-side.

* To make the correct passing decision
  when in possession.

* To read off the front attacking player and
  other attackers in the practice.

* To create options for the ball carrier.

* To use the straight line option where
  possible.

Progressions and Differentiation

A defender may pick up a player on a one on
one mark.

Move to a line after offloading the ball.

Task/Group Organization

Work in a quarter of the court in a 4v2 with
two static feeders at each end.

The ball starts with a feeder and all players
touch a line, then offer for the ball.

Attackers make at least four passes before
passing to the other feeder.

To restart the practice, the attack will then
move to touch a line and repeat.

Work four repetitions.

Potential Question to Pose

How can the attacker create space for another
player?

(Answer: Draw the defender by leading for
the ball and not remaining static.)

PRACTICE: TWO OFFERS
NUMBERS: EIGHT TO TEN

Attacking players are working out of two lines on a diagonal and must create two offers for the approaching ball carrier.

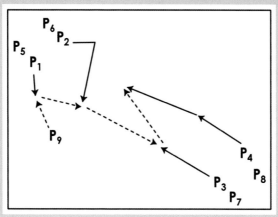

Practice Outcomes

* To use the straight line option where possible.

* To time the movement by reading off the approaching players.

* To pass ahead of the moving player with an appropriately weighted pass.

Progressions and Differentiation

Two players must make an additional pass before offloading the ball.

Add a floating defender and reduce the space.

Task/Group Organization

Work in half of the court on a diagonal with two lines formed at each point.

Two simultaneous offers from the line are made, with the non-receiver making a second offer to receive the ball (P2).

P2 should be ahead of the ball carrier to receive.

P3 and P4 provide two offers for P2 and P1 and P2 join the opposite line.

Move the ball for twenty passes.

Potential Question to Pose

If the attacker has not moved ahead of you as ball carrier, what type of pass is required?

(Answer: Lofted pass.)

PRACTICE: OFFERS AND OPTIONS 1
NUMBERS: EIGHT TO TWELVE

Attacking players are working out of two lines on a diagonal and must create two offers for the approaching ball carrier, with an option to pass back.

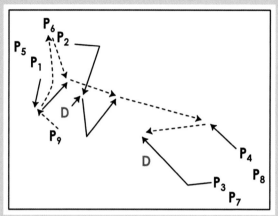

Practice Outcomes

* To use the straight line option where possible.

* To move and pass to ball-side.

* To make the correct decision related to when to pass and to whom.

* To time the movement by reading off the approaching players.

* To pass ahead of the moving player with an appropriately weighted pass.

Progressions and Differentiation

On a call of 'possession', the two players must move the ball on a 2v2 (four passes) before the two offers are made in the opposite line.

Task/Group Organization

As practice 'Two Offers', but add two defenders floating in the space.

There is an option now to pass back to a player in the line if the defence prevents a forwards pass to P2.

P1 here passes back to P6, as P2 is marked (P1 executes a double play).

P2 then re-offers up the court, with P3 and P4 offering from the opposite line.

Potential Question to Pose

Why might an attacker move close to the defender (zero phase)?

(Answer: To close off their movement if covering a space and to be ball-side).

PRACTICE: OFFERS AND OPTIONS 2
NUMBERS: SIX

Attacking players must move the ball through the court while the defence moves in a restricted space.

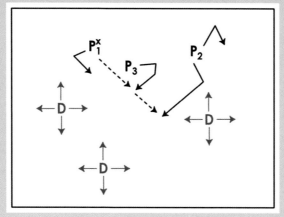

Practice Outcomes

* To use the straight line option where possible.

* To move and pass to ball-side.

* To close off the defender from ball-side by marking up close (zero phase).

* To use a double lead to commit and outwit the defence.

Task/Group Organization

3v3 in a half of a third area.

Defence can only move in the directions indicated above.

P1–3 move the ball through the space using a flat pass.

There must be two offers each time and six passes must be made to score.

On an interception the defence attempts four passes to score a point.

Progressions and Differentiation

Reduce the area (harder for attacking).

Remove a defender (easier).

No restriction on defender movement (harder).

Potential Question to Pose

When might a player choose to protect a space and use a hold?

(Answer: With a dominant defender who has speed and good reactions.)

PRACTICE: ATTACK CHALLENGE
NUMBERS: SIX

**Attacking players must use a different attacking move when approaching
a marker and offload to a feeder when all have received a pass.**

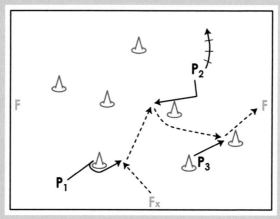

Practice Outcomes

* To use a range of attacking moves when getting free.

* To move towards the ball carrier on the straight line to receive.

* To clear as a front player to create space for others.

* To communicate on attack and read the cues to indicate readiness to receive a pass.

Progressions and Differentiation

Feeders move around the outside.

After one rotation of six passes a feeder comes in to be a defender.

Task/Group Organization

Use a half of a third area.

Six to eight markers are randomly placed.

Three static feeders around the outside of the practice space.

Three attacking players show different attacking moves at the markers, not repeating one in succession (30 seconds).

After all have received it, the ball goes to a feeder and the front player must clear (P2 above).

Potential Question to Pose

Where should the front player clear?

(Answer: Away from the other attackers and not in the line of the next intended pass.)

PRACTICE: TRANSITION NUMBERS: SIX

A 3v3 where players must demonstrate fast reactions on a transition from attack to defence.

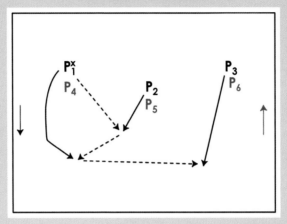

Practice Outcomes

* To move the ball at speed, applying the attacking principles of the straight line and ball-side.

* To make the transition from attack to defence at speed.

* To manage the transition phase and to select safe passing options.

* To devise a strategy when gaining possession that utilizes the strengths of the players.

Task/Group Organization

Use a half of a third area.

3v3 and each team moves the ball to their scoring end of the space (see arrows above).

On the command 'change', the ball must be dropped and the opposing team picks up and continues.

Work for 45 seconds, then rest.

Rotate the groups of three working.

Progressions and Differentiation

Feeders move around the outside.

After one rotation of six passes a feeder comes in to a defender.

Potential Question to Pose

What strategy might be used on the transition?

(Answer: Square the first pass to allow players time to reset/reposition.)

PRACTICE: FAKE THE PASS
NUMBERS: SIX

Players in possession attempt to deceive the defender and pass to the free player.

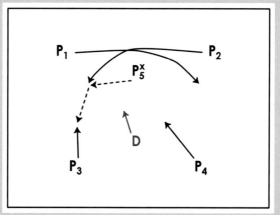

Practice Outcomes

* To deceive the defender by using the eyes, body or ball to outwit.

* To offload the ball to the free player.

* Players to offer for the ball moving toward the ball carrier.

Progressions and Differentiation

After the fake and pass to a player in the opposite line there must be four passes on a 2v1 (for example, P3 and P4 versus the defender) before the restart.

Task/Group Organization

Use a half of a third area.

P1 and P2 interchange.

P2 receives and must use the eyes, body or ball to deceive the defender.

P2 must select the best passing option with P3 and P4 offering.

Repeat with D becoming P5 and P3 and P4 on the interchange.

Always move back to the same line.

Potential Question to Pose

What can the body do to deceive the defender?

(Answer: Step towards or extend arms.)

PRACTICE: SWING THE BALL
NUMBERS: SEVEN

Two attacking players are pressurized on a 2v2 and must offer for the ball after a ball swing by the perimeter players.

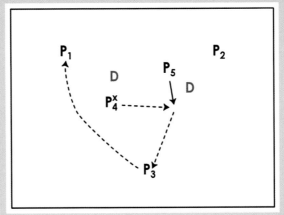

Practice Outcomes

* To use a double play to receive in a 2v2.

* To execute a fast take-off step to dominate and be ahead of the defender.

* To reposition after the ball swing and sight the other attacker at all times.

* To receive ball-side.

* To make effective decisions and use the post players if P4 and P5 are not free.

Progressions and Differentiation

Increase or decrease the number of passes required by P4 and P5.

Only one defender in the area (easier).

Task/Group Organization

Use a half of a third area.

Three static players and a 2v2 or 2v1 in the area.

P4 and P5 must receive three passes each to score a point; they can pass to P1–3, but this pass would not count.

When P1–3 receive the ball, they must swing it across to another static player (P3 to P1 above).

Work for 30 seconds, then rest.

Potential Question to Pose

As the ball swings, what must P4 and P5 do?

(Answer: Turn to face the direction of the pass and create a passing option.)

PRACTICE: TRIO TO GOAL
NUMBERS: SEVEN

Attacking players work the ball to goal, balancing the space whilst moving to the circle edge.

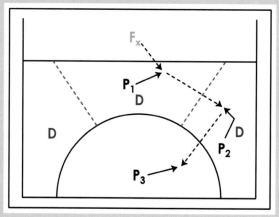

Practice Outcomes

* To balance the space whilst penetrating space to the circle edge.

* To receive ball-side and close off the defender.

* To pass the ball at speed and use a fast, flat pass where possible.

Progressions and Differentiation

Increase or decrease the defenders.

Defence can pick up one on one.

P3 can move out of the circle.

Task/Group Organization

Use a half-court area, working to goal.

3v3 and a static feeder (P3 works in the circle to receive).

P1–2 must be in a different channel.

Four passes outside of the shooting circle must occur before a shot at goal.

A defender can go into the circle.

Work for 30 seconds, rest and rotate positions.

Potential Question to Pose

What can a player do if they are not in a good position to receive on the circle edge?

(Answer: Move off and move again.)

PRACTICE: STRAIGHT LINE PLAY
NUMBERS: SIX

Attacking players work the ball to goal against two defenders aiming to pass on the straight line.

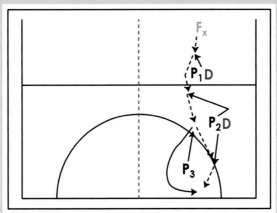

Practice Outcomes

* To balance the space while penetrating space to the circle edge.

* To receive ball-side and close off the defender.

* To pass on the straight line.

* To use a single or double lead to outwit the defender.

Task/Group Organization

Use a half-court area, working to goal.

3v2 and a static feeder (P3 works in and outside the circle to receive).

Four passes outside of the shooting circle must occur before a shot at goal.

A defender can go into the circle.

Work for 30 seconds, rest and rotate positions.

Progressions and Differentiation

Two players can enter the circle.

Condition the practice so that there must be a double play.

Potential Question to Pose

How should an attacking player land on the circle edge?

(Answer: For balance, use a wider than shoulder-width base.)

PRACTICE: RUN AT DEFENCE
NUMBERS: SEVEN

Attacking players must work the ball through the court against an overload of defence who space-mark.

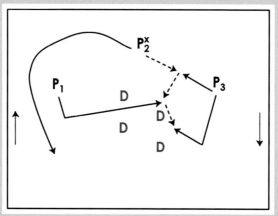

Practice Outcomes

* To balance the space while penetrating through the court.

* To receive ball-side and close off the defender.

* To look for a forward option as a priority.

* To look for opportunities to use a double play.

* To ensure there are two offers for the ball carrier.

Task/Group Organization

Use a half-court area, working to goal.

Four defenders space-mark and are restricted to a set area.

Four passes must be made before reaching the goal line.

A defender can go into the circle.

Work for 30 seconds, rest and rotate attack with defence.

Progressions and Differentiation

Defence go one on one with a defender floating for flying intercepts.

Introduce a shooting opportunity.

Potential Question to Pose

How can the three attackers outwit the overloaded defence?

(Answer: First mover pulls defence in or apart ready for the second offer.)

PRACTICE: PRECISION PASS AND MOVE
NUMBERS: EIGHT+

Players use a range of attacking moves to receive a pass.

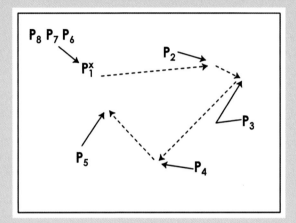

Practice Outcomes

* To employ a range of attacking moves with speed and precision timing.

* To place the ball effectively ahead of the receiver.

* To evaluate the speed and range of extension for each player.

* To assess when and where to pass the ball based upon the strengths of the receiver.

Task/Group Organization

Use a half-court area with five points to start the practice and work clockwise.

P1 uses a straight lead, P2 leads to the back space for a lob, P3 executes a double lead, P4 uses a straight lead for a flat pass and P5 is jogging in the space, then uses a straight lead to receive.

Players move on to the next point after passing the ball.

Work for four circuits.

Progressions and Differentiation

Add defence and reduce the space.

Introduce a shooting opportunity.

Potential Question to Pose

What cues should the ball carrier look for?

(Answer: Ball carrier speed of release or speed of the receiver.)

PRACTICE: TRANSITION CHALLENGE
NUMBERS: EIGHT

Team challenge in which both teams pass and move, with a team making the transition to defend the other team if their colour is called.

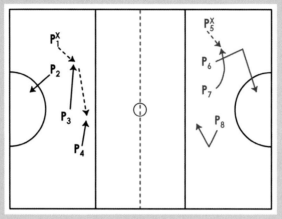

Practice Outcomes

* To execute an effective transition from attack to defence.

* To devise a strategy to counteract the defending team.

* The attacking team must describe the strategy used by the defence to try to counteract their play.

Task/Group Organization

4v4 with bibs work for 30 seconds.

After the call, the defending team must pass their ball to the coach and defend to deny the other team getting the ball to the line.

Eight spot markers can be placed at the half-way point and when a team scores they take a marker to their goal line (indicates who is in the lead).

Progressions and Differentiation

Both teams pass and move in the same area (harder).

Add a support player on the sideline who can support the attacking team.

Potential Question to Pose

What should the attacking team do to deceive the defence in this practice?

(Answer: Three offers: long, mid and short so as to split the defence.)

PRACTICE: MULTI-LEADS
NUMBERS: FIVE

Players must use a range of double leads passing and receiving at speed in a specific court area.

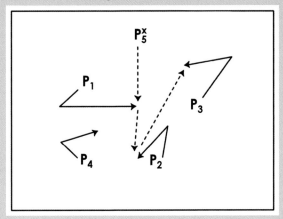

Practice Outcomes

* To employ a range of double leads.

* To place the ball effectively ahead of the receiver.

* To select a double lead not executed by the previous mover.

* To assess when and where to pass the ball and balance the space at all times.

* All players must continually offer, but may not receive.

Progressions and Differentiation

Players must touch a line after passing the ball (higher intensity and work rate).

Employ a set passing order.

Task/Group Organization

Work in a half of a third area and work towards and from the goal.

Players should be grouped in their units and work in a relevant area of the court.

Work for 30 seconds, then rest.

Players can use a range of double leads: for example up and back, forwards to right or left.

Potential Question to Pose

What may impact upon the timing of the pass?

(Answer: The time taken by the receiver to change direction.)

PRACTICE: MULTI-LEAD COMBO NUMBERS: NINE TO EIGHTEEN

Players must use a range of double leads passing and receiving at speed in a specific area while moving the ball through the court to the next group.

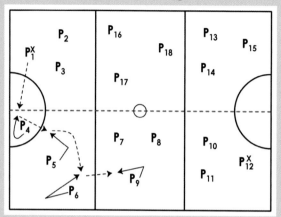

Practice Outcomes

* To employ a range of double leads.

* To place the ball effectively ahead of the receiver.

* To assess when and where to pass the ball and balance the space at all times.

* To open up a player's vision so as to be able to see the movements of players in the next third.

* To pass the ball into the next third using a straight-line option.

Task/Group Organization

Work in a half- third area with three to six groups.

Players should be grouped in their units and work in a relevant area of the court.

All players must receive in their area.

The ball is moved around all groups anticlockwise as in the diagram.

Two netballs in the practice.

Each ball should make two rotations around the court and each group of three.

Progressions and Differentiation

Players are allowed to keep the ball in their area if no straight-line option available.

A player could move into the next group and defend (3v1 situation).

Potential Question to Pose

What should a player do in the game if a forwards option is not available?

(Answer: Square ball on the overlap.)

PRACTICE: 2v2 PRESSURE
NUMBERS: EIGHT

A 2v2 situation where players execute only single leads to receive, with an option to interchange with a static player outside the defined area.

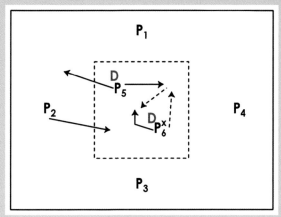

Practice Outcomes

* To perform single leads to receive.

* To place the ball ahead of the receiver.

* To assess when and where to pass the ball and balance the space at all times.

* To interchange with a static player if unable to get free for a pass.

* To move ball-side of the defence to receive a pass and no overhead passes.

Task/Group Organization

Work in a half of a third area.

Static players are positioned around the outside and will interchange if the attacker cannot get free (3-second rule).

The player to interchange is the one closest to the attacker as they move out of the 2v2 space.

P5 and P6 in the illustration will aim for six passes without interruption, repeat and then change roles.

Progressions and Differentiation

As the attacker moves out, any static player can move in to receive.

Could be a 3v2 to make the practice easier for the attackers.

Potential Question to Pose

If a player cannot get free, where should they exit the 2v2 area?

(Answer: Away from ball-side to open up space for the interchanging player.)

PRACTICE: RANDOM SPACES
NUMBERS: SIX

Players must be moving into a free space in order to receive the ball.

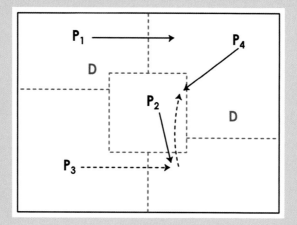

Practice Outcomes

* To perform single leads to receive.

* To place the ball ahead of the receiver.

* To use peripheral vision to sight the attacking and defending players.

* To move ball-side of the defence to receive a pass and no overhead passes.

* To receive the pass on the move.

Progressions and Differentiation

Defence could pick up one on one to pressure the more able players.

No overhead passes by the attackers.

Task/Group Organization

Work in a half of a third area.

Five spaces are defined and the defence can move freely into each space to pressure the attack.

Players should be moving at all times and show an accelerated pace when moving to receive.

Only one attacking player per space at all times.

Aim for twelve uninterrupted passes.

Potential Question to Pose

How can the attackers working with a player be supported?

(Answer: Keep moving in the space and the defence must work hard to sight all movers.)

PRACTICE: GATE CHALLENGE
NUMBERS: EIGHT TO TEN

Attacking players pass and move around the circle edge with an overload of defensive pressure.

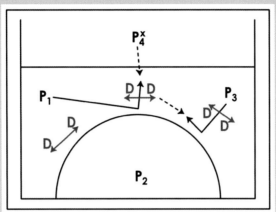

Practice Outcomes

* To move the ball from the centre third to the circle edge.

* To deliver a pass to the shooter, who is moving towards the goal.

* All circle-edge attack to move through a defensive gate prior to receiving a pass.

* To move assertively and at speed, reading and responding quickly to the defensive cues.

Progressions and Differentiation

If P2 misses, all attacking players must complete four shuttle runs across the third (raises intensity/pressure on P2).

P2 can move out of the circle also.

Task/Group Organization

Work in half-court area with the ball starting in the centre third.

A total of four gates must be moved through before P2 receives.

Defence can only move laterally and must remain in tandem (3m apart).

P2 is the shooter and stays in the circle, is constantly on the move and positioning ball-side.

P2 takes a shot and rebounds – repeat ×4.

Potential Question to Pose

How can the attack deceive the defence here?

(Answer: Two offers or swing the ball across the court.)

CHAPTER 4

DECISION-TRAINING PRACTICES FOR COACHING SHOOTING

There are several shooting styles across the world, but the preferred technique has changed from a two-handed shot to the one-handed high release shot. Australian shooting legend Margaret Caldow devised the one-handed high release technique that now dominates the game. It must be noted that the Caribbean nations follow the technique implemented by Trinidadian shooter Jean Pierre who played at international level and competed in five consecutive world championships. In this Caribbean style the shooting arm starts much lower than the Australian style, but is released at a similar point. The stance is different, with the Caribbean shot having the shooting foot placed forwards with weight on the back foot, in contrast to the Australian stance being parallel with feet shoulder-width apart.

It is the Australian high release shot that is adopted and coached within the development and international programmes in the UK. This style allows a shooter to clear the ball away from a defender and in the preparation phase the shooter should note the following technical points:

The goal shooter chooses to protect the goal attack from the reach of the goal keeper.

* Body balanced with feet hip-width apart and back straight.
* Ball held high above the head with the ball resting on the fingers of the shooting hand.
* Wrist under the ball and fingers should face backwards.
* The second hand is used to steady the ball by positioning on the side of the ball.
* Eyes focused on the front of the ring and ball to be lifted above this point.

At the execution phase:
* Wrist should drop slightly behind the head.
* Use the index finger to guide the shot with a little backspin.
* Use knees and ankles to push ball upwards and forwards to goal.
* The ball should lift high over the front of the ring and for a clean shot should begin to drop into the goal at the midpoint above the ring.

The high release point for the shot.

In the follow-through the index finger should point forwards and slightly downwards. A shooter may use their footwork skills and use the rules to their advantage by implementing a step backwards, forwards or to the side when in the act of shooting. If a defender is placing a great deal of pressure on the shooter the step backwards and to the side can counteract this pressure and give the shooter more space to release the ball. Such steps can also be used when throwing the ball to relieve pressure being forced on the shooter by the defender and gain an advantage.

The step forwards is used when the defender is not positioned in front, allowing the shooter the chance to move closer to the post. This is most commonly seen in a penalty shot situation when the opponent is stood by the shooter's side until the ball is released.

Once the basic shooting technique has been mastered, a player can begin to use the step. When executing the step it is vital that the body weight is rebalanced over the leading foot. Balance must be maintained throughout the action and follow-through.

> **Tips for Shooting**
> * Follow the Australian technique.
> * Master the technique by practising daily.
> * Body balance is crucial.
> * Use the stepping techniques to gain an advantage.
> * Remember the landing foot when using the step techniques.

Netball rules permit only two players to shoot in a match, these being the goal attack and goal shooter, hence it is vital that they have a high-percentage success rate. A shooter must have confidence in their ability and must have the qualities to cope well under pressure.

HINTS FOR SUCCESS AS A SHOOTER

A shooter must be prepared to practise frequently until all actions of the shot become automatic. Practising from a range of areas in the shooting circle is the key to success, as well as the shooter knowing their own personal high-percentage scoring spots. Shooting practice should simulate the nature of the game and executing shots under pressure, with limited time and with distractions, will provide a relevant training environment. When shooting further away from the post, the shot must have an increased follow-through.

A shooter should engage in decision-making and analyse each shot they take in practice by asking questions such as: Was the shot too short? Did the shot

Focus by the shooter is essential under pressure.

Goal shooter demonstrating strength to extend and catch the ball under pressure.

have too much power? Was I off balance? A shooter must know:

* When to shoot and when to pass.
* What options are available both in and outside the shooting circle.
* How much space is available within the circle.
* Where the defence is located.
* Where the circle-edge feeders are.
* Where the other shooter is located.
* What the strengths and weaknesses of the defence pairing in the circle are.

A shooter can quickly evaluate her defender in the first few minutes of the game, then work to expose further her weaknesses and limit her strengths. Below are some examples of situations a shooter may face:

Defender is strong on the left side and sets up her defence looking to her left: Shooter needs to keep her feet moving, making her movements crisp, and lead strongly to the right side of the court. Preliminary moves should be used to drag the defender over to the left, so that the shooter has room to lead to the right. The shooter could also communicate with the other shooter and wing attack, indicating that she will take the right-hand side leads and enter the circle more on this side.

Defender fully commits to the interception of the first ball: The shooter needs to keep her leads strong on to the ball, using a variety of leads and dodges, with movements being concise. A very strong drive on to the ball will ensure that the defender goes with the shooter and the defender will be committed to intercept. An astute feeder may fake the ball, sucking the defender in and assisting the shooter to drop back to the space by holding the pass until the shooter has changed direction.

Defender is tall and very good on any high ball: The shooter must work the ground and use her concise dodges, leads and breaks (direction change).

Front cuts and working in front will be a valuable option. Leads that require a high ball or lob, especially in the circle, should be avoided. A short shooter against a tall defender is a viable option, especially if she can work the ball around quickly and effectively. Rebound opportunities may be limited, so accuracy is very important.

Goal defence sits back in the circle to double-defend the tall goal shooter: A good strategy is that the goal attack gets in the circle also. This will make the defenders pick up a shooter each. If the circle defence are not 1 v 1 marking, then the goal attack is free to shoot.

A shooter must commit fully to practise over and above that of her teammates, given the responsibility held for scoring the goals. Ensuring practices simulate the game pressures and overall range of decisions a shooter must make will contribute to the development of a successful performance in this role.

PRACTICE: SHOOTER MOVES
NUMBERS: FOUR

The shooter must move around the markers before receiving a pass and executing the shot.

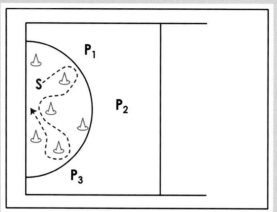

Practice Outcomes

*   To move efficiently around the markers, maintaining an upright body position.

*   To move to a different-coloured marker each time.

*   To use and change the body angle to sight the ball at all times.

*   To use a strong take-off on the change of direction.

*   To execute a shot at the end of the sprint to the post.

Task/Group Organization

Work in the goal circle and use six markers of varying colours.

P1–P3 pass the ball continuously.

P1–P3 can pass to the shooter at any point and when moving to the post.

The shooter should cover at least two markers before receiving the ball.

If the shooter gets the rebound another shot can be executed – repeat ×6.

Work for 30 seconds.

Progressions and Differentiation

Defenders can shadow in the circle.

Another shooter can be added.

P1–3 complete four passes in the third before a pass to the shooter.

Potential Question to Pose

What makes a good body angle when moving between markers?

(Answer: Upper body should face the ball so as to be able to see most of the space at all times.)

PRACTICE: SHOOTER ROTATION
NUMBERS: FIVE

Two shooters are balancing the space and receiving the ball from a passer in the front space.

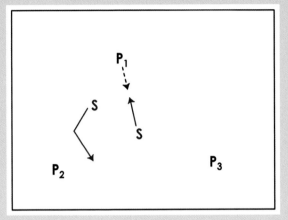

Practice Outcomes

* To read off the front shooter and balance the space.

* To ensure that the shooter moves towards the ball carrier to receive.

* To recognize the front mover as P1–P3 pass to each other.

* To execute a clearing move by avoiding moving across the line of the ball.

Task/Group Organization

Work in a triangle format with the three passers (goal circle if possible).

P1–P3 can pass the ball between themselves.

The ball should be passed to a shooter as they move towards the ball carrier.

Work for 30–40 seconds.

Progressions and Differentiation

A defender can shadow and deny space.

Shooter takes a shot each time, or must pass to the other before a shot is taken.

Potential Question to Pose

When the ball is passed from P1 to P3 what must the shooters do?

(Answer: Quickly reposition to see the ball and the back must read off the front shooter.)

PRACTICE: SHOOTER TWO ON TWO
NUMBERS: SEVEN

Two shooters are attempting to outwit the defence and receive a pass ball-side inside the goal circle.

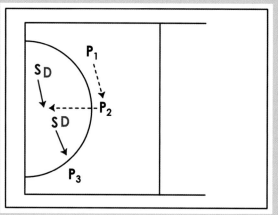

Practice Outcomes

* To read off the front shooter and balance the space.

* To move to receive in a ball-side position.

* To balance the space within the goal circle.

* To score goals.

* To sight the ball at all times.

Progressions and Differentiation

Only one defender in the practice.

Shooter must execute a shooter to shooter ball before the shot.

Task/Group Organization

Two shooters and two defence in the circle (work for 30 seconds).

P1–P3 can pass to each other on the edge of the circle or into a shooter.

The shooter can elect to shoot or pass.

The ball cannot be passed out to P1–3 until a shot has been executed.

Whoever gains possession passes the ball to either P1-3 but not the P who last touched the ball.

Potential Question to Pose

What can the shooter do to outwit the defender and create space?

(Answer: Assertive movement, use the whole circle area to pull the defence apart.)

PRACTICE: SHOOTER WIDE
NUMBERS: FIVE

Two shooters move around the markers, balancing the space and receiving while moving towards the post.

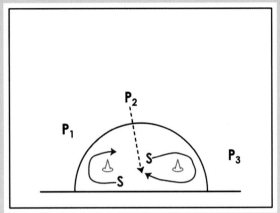

Practice Outcomes

* To read off the front shooter and balance the space.

* To move and receive a flat, fast pass on a lead towards the post.

* To maintain vision on the ball.

* To score goals.

* To sight the ball at all times.

Task/Group Organization

Two shooters work around two wide markers in the circle.

P1–P3 can pass to each other on the edge of the circle or into a shooter.

The shooter can elect to shoot or pass.

The ball cannot be passed out to P1–3 until a shot has been executed.

Whoever gains possession after the shot passes back to a passer, but not the one who passed into a shooter.

Progressions and Differentiation

Add a defender in the practice.

Add two more markers at the top of the circle and near the post for four directions to rotate around.

Potential Question to Pose

What must the shooters do to communicate effectively?

(Answer: Use their vision to see each other when moving wide.)

PRACTICE: SHOOTER TOP AND BASE NUMBERS: FIVE

Two shooters move around the markers balancing the space receiving while moving towards the post.

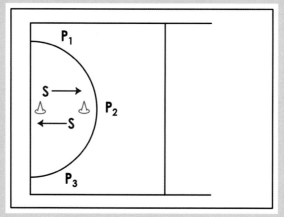

Practice Outcomes

* To read off the front shooter and balance the space.

* To move and receive a flat fast pass on a lead towards the post.

* To maintain vision on the ball.

* To score goals.

* To sight the ball at all times.

* To sprint through the middle section of the markers to hit the top of the circle.

Task/Group Organization

Two shooters work around two markers in the circle (top and base).

P1–P3 can pass to each other on the edge of the circle or into a shooter.

The shooter can elect to shoot or pass.

The ball cannot be passed out to P1–3 until a shot has been executed.

Whoever gains possession after the shot passes back to a passer but not the one who passed into a shooter.

Progressions and Differentiation

Add a defender in the practice.

Allow P1–3 to make four passes starting in the centre third before a pass to the shooter.

Potential Question to Pose

What must the back shooter be aware of?

(Answer: The front shooter who might change the direction of the movement and the location of the ball.)

PRACTICE: FOUR POINT ROTATION
NUMBERS: FIVE

**Two shooters move around the markers balancing the space receiving
while moving towards the post.**

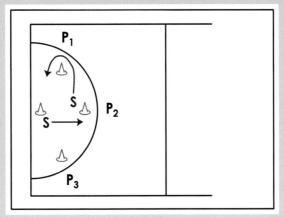

Practice Outcomes

* To read off the front shooter and balance the space.

* To move and receive a flat fast pass on a lead towards the post.

* To maintain vision on the ball.

* To score goals.

* To sight the ball at all times.

Task/Group Organization

Two shooters work around four markers in the circle.

P1–P3 can pass to each other on the edge of the circle or into a shooter.

The shooter can elect to shoot or pass.

The ball cannot be passed out to P1–3 until a shot has been executed.

Whoever gains possession after the shot passes back to a passer but not the one who passed into a shooter.

Progressions and Differentiation

Add a defender in the practice.

Allow P1–3 to make four passes starting in the centre third before a pass to the shooter.

Potential Question to Pose

What position should the two shooters try not to be in?

(Answer: Side by side, as difficult to read and know who the lead player should be.)

PRACTICE: SHOOTER PEPPER POT
NUMBERS: FOUR

A shooter must work at a game intensity, receiving a set number of passes before executing a shot.

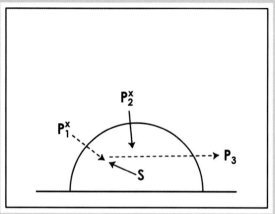

Practice Outcomes

* To score goals after working at a high intensity within the goal circle.

* To receive a flat, fast pass.

* To react quickly after releasing the ball and move to collect the next pass.

* To execute a single lead for the ball at speed.

* To shoot under pressure after a high workload.

Task/Group Organization

P1 and P2 start with a ball.

Shooter must receive eight passes and as soon as the shooter passes the ball the next one is thrown into the circle.

After the eight passes the shooter takes three shots at goal from differing points.

The shooter must pass the ball to a free passer (P3 in the illustration).

The shooter cannot pass back to the passer who delivered the ball.

Progressions and Differentiation

Add a defender in the practice.

P1–3 to defend the three shots.

P1–3 could pass to each other to change the passer without a ball.

Potential Question to Pose

What should the shooter focus on while moving?

(Answer: Sight P1–3 and the both netballs whenever possible.)

PRACTICE: STEP-CHANGE NUMBERS: TWO

A shooter simulates movements used in the game and must execute either a standing, step-back or to-the-side shooting action.

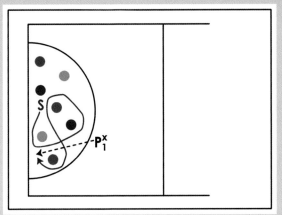

Practice Outcomes

* To score goals after working at a high intensity within the goal circle.

* To execute a shot using either the step-back or step to-the-side action.

* To use a strong change of direction at the markers.

* To move around three different colours before receiving a pass from P1.

* To pass to a shooter moving towards the post.

Progressions and Differentiation

Add a defender in the practice.

P1 can challenge for the rebound.

Increase the number of markers the shooter must move to.

Task/Group Organization

Red, green and blue markers (×7).

Shooter must move to three different-coloured markers before shooting.

If the shooter lands near a green marker the shot must be a step-to-the-side; if red a step-back action and if blue it should be a standing shot.

Two pairs can work in each goal circle to add pressure in locating a free marker.

Potential Question to Pose

When would a shooter use the step-back or step-to-the-side action?

(Answer: When the defender has a long reach over the ball.)

PRACTICE: SCREEN START
NUMBERS: FOUR

Two shooters move out to the markers and back to the midpoint in the shooting circle, setting a screen when possible.

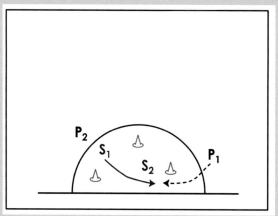

Practice Outcomes

* To sprint to the markers and post at a high intensity.

* To simulate setting a screen to close off a defender.

* To maintain quality vision by sighting the other shooter at all times.

* To read off the front shooter when on the move.

Progressions and Differentiation

Add a defender in the practice, working at 50 per cent.

P1 and P2 can pass the ball to each other.

Task/Group Organization

Three markers placed at the top, left and right of the circle.

Both shooters move around the markers, balancing the space.

Either shooter will call 'screen', which is S2 in the illustration and S1 then moves behind S2 to receive the pass from P1.

Ball is passed out to the other P to restart the practice.

Potential Question to Pose

When is a screen often used?

(Answer: To open up space for a fellow teammate, when defence is positioned away from ball-side.)

PRACTICE: GIVE–GO–SHOOT
NUMBERS: FOUR

Two shooters work to balance the circle and move to opposing colour markers while two players bring the ball to the circle edge.

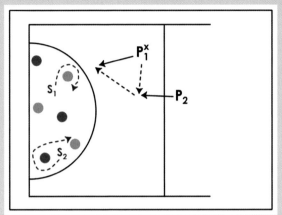

Practice Outcomes

* To maintain quality vision by sighting the other shooter at all times.

* To read off the front shooter when on the move.

* To create a goal-scoring opportunity by receiving the ball near the post.

* To anticipate the direction of movement of the front shooter.

Progressions and Differentiation

Add a defender in the practice.

Condition: the shooter must pass out and receive again prior to a shot.

Task/Group Organization

Six markers placed in the goal circle.

Both shooters move around the markers balancing the space.

The second mover must move to a different-coloured marker, for example, if S1 moves to green, S2 must move to red whilst balancing the circle.

The ball is passed to a shooter from the circle edge and a shot taken; the ball is passed back to P1 to restart.

Potential Question to Pose

When should the front shooter clear?

(Answer: When they arrive in the front space too early or they are tightly marked.)

PRACTICE: WHAT COLOUR?
NUMBERS: THREE

A shooter works on the speed of movement leading into the goal circle, whilst maintaining their vision to call out the colour held up by 'P'

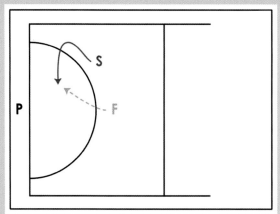

Practice Outcomes

* To execute a single lead into the goal circle to receive a pass.

* To execute a running shot and collect the rebound.

* To enter the goal circle from the top and side positions at speed.

* To demonstrate visual awareness by seeing more than just the ball.

Task/Group Organization

Three coloured markers or pieces of card are needed.

Shooter starts with the ball and distributes to the feeder (F), moving into the goal circle to receive a pass and execute a running shot.

At the same time the shooter must call out the colour of the marker being held up in the air by P.

Progressions and Differentiation

Add a defender in the practice.

Shooter must receive six passes and call all colour changes before taking a shot.

Potential Question to Pose

What body position helps to maintain good vision?

(Answer: Look ahead, head up and upper body upright.)

PRACTICE: BASELINE CHALLENGE? NUMBERS: THREE

A shooter attempts to outwit the defender, while moving to points on the baseline prior to receiving a pass and executing the shot.

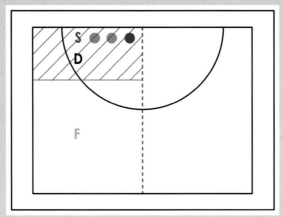

Practice Outcomes

* To use a change of direction to outwit the defender.

* To receive a fast, flat pass on the baseline.

* To assess the defender strengths and weaknesses when tracking.

* To take a shot and compete for the rebound.

Progressions and Differentiation

Shooter scores two points for a goal if they reach the red marker.

Shooter must receive two passes from F before a shot.

Task/Group Organization

Three coloured markers (two green and two red as in the illustration) ×4 reps.

The shooter must travel to four cones from the start point before receiving a pass and shooting (stay in the defined area).

The defender will mark the shot and compete for the rebound.

Two points if the pass is not overhead from F, one point for a goal and one for the rebound.

Potential Question to Pose

What technical skill might be useful for the shooter here to outwit the defender?

(Answer: Sell a dummy, feint dodge.)

PRACTICE: CIRCLE DRIVE
NUMBERS: THREE

Two shooters pass the ball outside of the circle and moving into the goal circle with a defender attempting to delay, deny and gain possession.

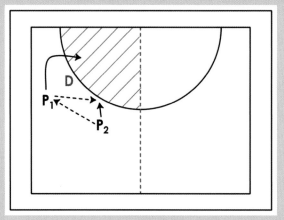

Practice Outcomes

* To prevent the defender being between the ball carrier and receiver.

* To pass the ball flat and fast, moving outside of the circle.

* To use a front cut to ensure the defender is not ball-side.

* To accelerate into the goal circle for a shooting opportunity.

* To feed the ball from the circle edge.

Task/Group Organization

Use half of the goal circle 2v1.

Five passes must be made outside of the circle before one shooter enters.

If the defender is between P1 and P2 the pass is not counted in the five.

The defender tries to delay the shooter entering (shooter has 3 seconds to enter and receive).

Shooter collects rebound, pass to P and restart (work for five reps).

Progressions and Differentiation

Defender marks the shot.

P1 and P2 start at the centre-third line.

Use the full goal circle (easier for the attackers).

Potential Question to Pose

How can you outwit the defender on the circle edge?

(Answer: Use all the available space, one shooter draws the defender and the other enters the circle.)

PRACTICE: SHOOTER HIGH OR LOW NUMBERS: THREE

The three attacking players work the ball through the court to a shooting opportunity, with all players reacting to the set-up position of GS.

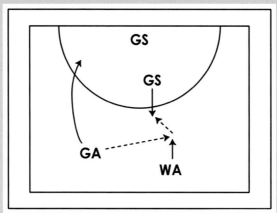

Practice Outcomes

* To ensure court balance and communication between shooters.

* To pass the ball flat and fast, moving towards the circle edge.

* To ensure that the goal attack enters the circle at the correct point, given the goal shooter set-up.

* To select the best passing option based upon the set-up of the goal shooter.

Progressions and Differentiation

Add the centre position and work from the centre pass.

Add a floating defender.

Task/Group Organization

Goal third area and practice starts with wing attack, who throws the ball up and turns to face the goal.

The goal shooter randomly changes the start position either high or low in the circle.

Five passes must be made before a shot is taken.

The rebound should be retrieved by a shooter.

Repeat × 5.

Potential Question to Pose

When the goal shooter is high, what should the goal attack do?

(Answer: Look to enter on a baseline run, look for a pass from the goal shooter moving towards the post.)

PRACTICE: SHOOTER FEED
NUMBERS: SEVEN

The shooter works with two circle-edge players to pass and look for a high-percentage shooting opportunity after receiving three passes.

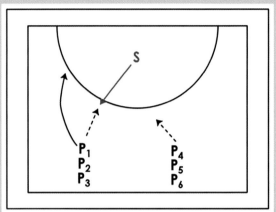

Practice Outcomes

* To set an attacking triangle between the three players.

* To lead for the ball at game intensity.

* To turn fully upon receiving the ball to sight both passing options.

* To select the best passing option based upon the set-up of the two circle-edge players.

* To use the straight-line pass whenever possible.

Progressions and Differentiation

Add a defender in the circle and/or one covering the circle edge.

Move the lines of players back to the centre-third area for more passes.

Task/Group Organization

Two lines of players in the goal third with one shooter in the goal circle.

P1 and P2 would support the shooter on the first repetition (see illustration).

Three passes must be received before a shot is taken.

The rebound should be retrieved.

Repeat × 5 and change the shooter.

Potential Question to Pose

What are the benefits of turning to face the goal as the shooter?

(Answer: Readiness to shoot, defender could be deceived by anticipating the shot when the shooter plans to pass.)

PRACTICE: BEAT THE BOX-OUT NUMBERS: TWO

The shooter takes shots from various points in the outer circle and must then complete for the rebound with the defender, who will box out after the shot.

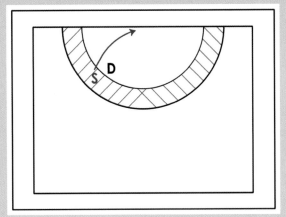

Practice Outcomes

* To achieve a shooting success rate of 80 per cent+ from the outer circle.

* To use the fake on the shot to outwit the defender.

* To beat the defender to the post and/or collect the rebound.

* To assess the strengths and weaknesses of the defender in order to counteract.

Task/Group Organization

A shooter and defender in the circle with the outer circle defined for the practice (markers may be used).

The shooter must shoot from a different point each time and compete to get to the post and/or collect the rebound.

If the shooter rebounds she should take the shot.

Repeat ×10, aiming for 8/10 or more.

Progressions and Differentiation

Add a feeder on the edge so that the shooter must receive a pass and shoot on a 1v1.

Potential Question to Pose

When would a shooter fake the shot in this situation?

(Answer: To commit the defender to perhaps jump or fall in on the shot.)

PRACTICE: TOP FEED
NUMBERS: FOUR

The goal attack is working on a lead into the circle on a 1v1 and the feed must be from the top of the circle.

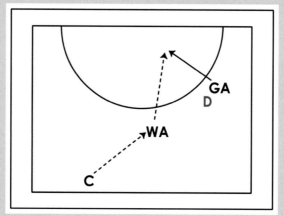

Practice Outcomes

*   To achieve a shooting success rate of 80 per cent or higher.

*   To receive a pass ball-side of the defender.

*   To offer and re-offer to create a suitable option for the ball carrier.

*   To receive a pass moving to the post.

*   To assess the strengths and weaknesses of the defender in order to counteract.

Progressions and Differentiation

Add another defender to create a 2v1 with the centre and wing attack.

Add the goal shooter and a defender into the practice.

Task/Group Organization

A goal attack and defender position on the outside of the circle edge.

A centre and wing attack bring the ball to the edge from the third line.

The shooter can use a range of skills to receive ball-side, for example front cut, straight lead or change of direction.

If the shooter rebounds she should take another shot.

Repeat × 5.

Potential Question to Pose

When would a shooter need to change direction to be ball-side?

(Answer: When the defender is faster, or has run out of court area available to receive a pass.)

PRACTICE: SPLIT THE CIRCLE
NUMBERS: FIVE

The shooter pairing is working to balance the circle and receive a pass moving at intensity towards the goal post.

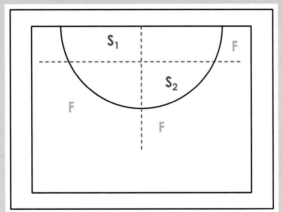

Practice Outcomes

* To achieve a shooting success rate of 80 per cent or higher.

* To receive a pass replicating game intensity and moving towards the post.

* To time the move to receive a pass on the first second from the circle-edge feeders.

* To balance the circle and ensure the head is up to maintain good vision of ball and players.

Task/Group Organization

Two shooters in the goal circle and three feeders on the circle edge.

Shooters must rotate and move at game intensity as the feeders pass the ball between themselves.

At any point the ball can go into a shooter.

A shooter should look for a pass to the other shooter if it creates an improved shooting option.

Progressions and Differentiation

The feeders can work the ball through the court on a 2v1 from the centre third.

Add a defender into the practice within the goal circle.

Potential Question to Pose

What position should the two shooters avoid?

(Answer: Both side by side or in a flat/parallel position.)

PRACTICE: GO FOR GOAL
NUMBERS: FOUR

The attacking unit work the ball through to goal on the straight line.

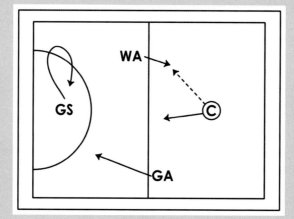

Practice Outcomes

* To achieve a shooting success rate of 80 per cent or higher.

* To receive a pass replicating game intensity and on a straight line.

* To ensure there are three options for the ball carrier at all times.

* To ensure the head is up to maintain good vision seeing ball and players.

* To ensure there is always an offer on the overlap.

Progressions and Differentiation

Add a defender into the practice within the goal circle or to hover around the circle edge.

Reduce the width of the court (easier).

Task/Group Organization

Four players take the positions of the attacking unit.

The practice starts at the centre pass and can go to either player, with a condition that the ball moves through on the straight line or the overlap can be used.

The coach can set conditions to promote decision-making, for example the goal defence is faster than the goal attack, or the ball must be flat into the shooters.

Potential Question to Pose

At what point should the shooter offer through the top of the circle?

(Answer: When the goal attack is not an option due to being wide or marked.)

PRACTICE: SHOOTER PROGRAMME NUMBERS: ONE TO TWO

Three examples of shooting tasks that can be offered as part of a shooter's daily routine when practising alone or with a partner at the post.

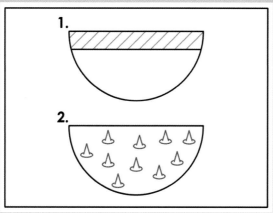

Practice Outcomes

* To achieve a shooting success rate of 80 per cent or higher.

* To shoot under pressure created by a penalty for the missed shot.

* To rebound all shots.

* To evaluate one's own shooting performance and make necessary adjustments for the successful outcome.

Task/Group Organization

Shooter executes twenty-five shots from anywhere in the shaded area, thinking about their technique and collecting the rebound (see diagram 1).

Shooter shoots × 5 shots from each marker. Place the cone outside of the court area when two shots are taken without the two misses to show success (see diagram 2).

Progressions and Differentiation

Reduce or raise the intensity prior to shooting in both tasks.

Shot taken must be a step back or step to the side.

Potential Question to Pose

How could personal accuracy in task two be described?

(Answer: For example, higher percentage success in the mid-range, weaker on the left side and so on.)

CHAPTER 5

DECISION-TRAINING PRACTICES FOR COACHING DEFENDING SKILLS

Each of the seven players on the court is required to defend and each must be able to demonstrate the ability to defend both on the receiver and on the ball. When marking the receiver, the defender must shadow the attacker and restrict and prevent her from moving into the desirable space. When defending on the ball, a player can influence the accuracy, direction, pace and height of the pass. By placing pressure on the ball, the defender should limit the options by restricting the ball carrier's vision to locate the mover and passing space.

In netball there are three stages of defence whereby a player makes attempts to gain an interception. When defending, a player should make a quick transition from one stage to the next, for example: one on one marking; pressure on the ball; and restricting the player. At all times the player is trying to gain possession by forcing the receiver or ball carrier into an error.

> **STAGES OF DEFENCE**
> **Stage One:** Marking a player without the ball.
> **Stage Two:** Marking a player in possession of the ball.
> **Stage Three:** Restricting the player's movement.

STAGE ONE DEFENCE

The aim of stage one defence is to mark a player closely to prevent them from receiving the ball or to gain an interception. If the ball is moving down the court a defender must constantly move around their opponent and reposition as the ball switches from side to side. The defender tries to ensure that their opponent is not an option for the ball carrier. When a player is moving to get free from a dead-ball situation, for example a centre pass or throw-in, the defender must shadow the attacker and position very close to this player. The defender in this stage will try to intercept, force an uncontrolled receipt of the ball, or force an out of court.

Key coaching points for stage one:
* Feet shoulder width-apart.
* Weight balanced on balls of the feet.
* Arms flexed at front or side of body.
* Head up.
* Watch player and ball with back to the player.
* Position within an arm's reach of the attacker.
* Half-cover the attacking player.
* Body slightly angled to player's uncovered side.

Excellent stage-two defence with strong arms over.

STAGE TWO DEFENCE

If an opponent receives the ball the defender must then put pressure on the ball carrier and mark the pass from a distance of 0.9m from the attacker's landing foot. Defenders will at times drop back from 0.9m to cover the immediate space near to the ball carrier. Therefore, the aim of stage two is to apply pressure and restrict the vision of the ball carrier. The defender will try to intercept the pass, to tip the ball or force a weak pass. There are two approaches within this stage and a defender must decide whether to: (a) keep their feet on the ground and cover the ball and space with their outstretched arms and hands; or (b) choose to cover the ball, but prepare to jump when the ball is released from the thrower. A defender who has good elevation and a well-timed jump will use approach (b) to try for an interception.

Circle defence will often use a combination of both approaches to try to force the shooters into making an error, while players defending through the court will prefer to keep their feet grounded so that they can recover and deny space should they not gain possession. A defender must read the cues from the passer and assess the best approach to implement by asking themselves the following questions:

* Is my opponent taller than me?
* Does my opponent release the ball from a low position?
* If I am unsuccessful in stage two can my player gain ground away from me and be a key option for her team?
* Does the shooter miss when I lean or when I jump?
* If I defend further back from 0.9m does this force a slower pass for my teammates to intercept?

The defender should influence the direction and height of the pass if an interception cannot be gained and this may allow an interception for a defender marking the receiver. Following an assessment of their opponent a defender will select the best arm position to cover the ball, the distance they should stand from their opponent and their shoulder/body alignment in relation to the ball carrier and receiver.

Key coaching points for stage two:
* Take up 0.9m in front of player as quickly as possible.
* One arm extended over the ball and one covering the main space.
* On the balls of the feet.

* Feet shoulder-width apart.
* Knees flexed if executing a jump to defend.
* Head up watching the ball and ball carrier's eyes.
* If jumping, anticipate the release point.
* Jump up and towards the player for the interception.

STAGE THREE DEFENCE

This stage is also known as restrictive marking and the aim is to prevent an opponent from moving to their desired space on the court. A successful stage three defender will ensure that the player does not have the freedom to move to a desired location and will also force them to a sideline and into a crowded space. If a defender can restrict the attacker and keep her away from ball-side, they will force the opposition to use diagonal passes, which are more easily intercepted. If a defender is not successful at stage two, they must quickly recover and ensure that they close down the space.

Contesting for the ball.

A defender must have good agility and use small running and shuffling steps to track and stay close to the player in this stage. The defender should angle their body to drive the player away from the key attacking space. After stage two the defender will be facing the player and not the ball, so it is vital that after moment-arily delaying the run of the attacker they turn to face the ball.

Key coaching points for stage three:
*   Feet shoulder-width apart.
*   Knees slightly flexed.
*   Head and eyes up.
*   Body angled to view player and the ball.
*   Use stage one defending stance.

Throughout each stage of defending the player is striving to gain an interception and for this to occur a player must make a judgment as to the correct time to take off for the intercept. Players should always seek opportunities to try for an interception and with good timing the frequency of a successful turnover will increase. The defender must also develop good vision in order to mark an opponent, but also be aware of the path of the ball and seek out an intercepting opportun-ity. This intercepting opportunity may require the player to drop off their own opponent and possibly move to another opponent or space. Deception on defence can trick the opposition into thinking that there is an attacking option not covered by the defender and by positioning away from the space and the opponent the defender makes a move for the interception.

DEFENDER DECISION-MAKING

A player can utilize a range of strategies to defend a player in relation to stage one, namely: (a) switching; (b) sagging off or dropping off; and (c) forcing wide, middle or up the court. Switching involves defending a different player and this would normally occur with two players, for example the wing defence and centre, or the goal keeper and goal defence. Sagging or dropping off is where a defending player drops back into an identified space and prepares to defend a player who may move into this area. Players cannot execute this tactic in isola-tion and a useful situation to use this strategy would be at a dead-ball situation like the sideline or centre pass. Finally, when forcing players wide, to the middle or up the court, a group of players is often working collect-ively to force either a diagonal or long ball.

It is vital that any coach designs practices to develop the qualities essential for defending in netball, which are clearly defined as: dominance; determination; risk-taking; assertiveness; and control under pressure.

PRACTICE: TRACK A CHANNEL
NUMBERS: EIGHT TO FOURTEEN

Players work in pairs and together to deny space, track attacking players to limit their options and create opportunities to gain possession or force errors.

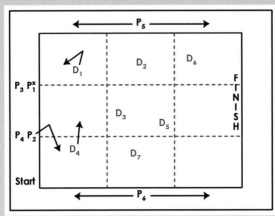

Practice Outcomes

*   To use stages of defence to limit attacking options and movement through the space.

*   To be ball-side and marking a player in their area.

*   To read others' intentions and be able to dictate and limit the options of attackers.

*   To read and attend to relevant cues.

Task/Group Organization

Use a third of the court area and only two defenders in a channel/area at any one time.

Attackers in twos (Ps) move ball through the area, nearest D to P1 stage-three mark and D4 move to get ball-side of P2 and stop the front cut.

P1 and P2 can pass to each other, but can use the other Ps.

Progressions and Differentiation

Attackers (P4 and P6 can move along line).

Defenders can double-mark in one channel.

Potential Question to Pose

What might the front defender do to outwit an attacker?

(Answer: Angle the body to see ball and player, be offline to disguise intention.)

PRACTICE: OFFLINE MARK NUMBERS: SIX TO TWELVE

Players work to intercept the ball through the passing lane, also reading perceptual and visual cues between thrower and attacker.

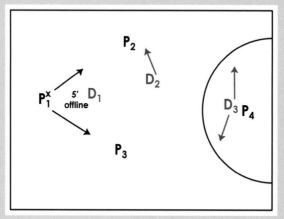

Practice Outcomes

* To be offline as a defender and limit passing options.

* To be able to show quick recovery and second-stage defending (arms over).

* To use tracking movements to deny the attacker.

* To be ball-side.

* To force the longest passing option so that defence can intercept.

Progressions and Differentiation

Another defender can drop into the goal circle.

Attackers can have limited amounts of passes before passing into goal circle.

Can open up the middle channel for attackers.

Task/Group Organization

Use middle channel of attacking third to goal.

Each defender to change roles (no bibs to overload the defenders in terms of their vision).

Start at P1, who has choice of passing to P2 or P3 (both static). D1 must be on 5 footmark and second stage; D2 to read and go for intercept or recover to second-stage defence.

If P2 receives, must work ball to P4 (D3 to be ball-side as ball is passed). Attackers target to get ball to P4 in goal circle.

Work for 30 seconds to 2 minutes.

Potential Question to Pose

What might defender 2 and 3 do to the non-ball carriers?

(Answer: Leave ball carrier and mark stage one on other attackers, mark around circle edge.)

PRACTICE: LEFT AND RIGHT FORCE NUMBERS: FIVE

Defenders must use stage-one defence and keep the front position, forcing the attacker to receive in the front area and instigating a long second pass.

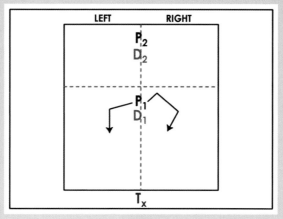

Practice Outcomes

* To keep front position on attacker.

* To stop the attacker using a front cut.

* To drop off an attacker and time the intercept.

* To use movements and body angles to set up for an interception.

* To use a change in pace.

Task/Group Organization

Use a half-court in width and length, making sure players work up and down.

Static thrower (T) passes to P1; P1 can go left or right side.

If P1 receives pass, they have to pass to P2 in to the back space of the area.

D2 will work to force (restrict) P2 to receive pass on opposite side (diagonal pass).

Progressions and Differentiation

Attackers can pass back to T and receive in opposite side (× 3 reps).

Add attackers and defenders to both sides, left and right.

Potential Question to Pose

When defender 1 has put P1 under pressure, what should D2 be doing?

(Answer: Sight the attacker, be ready to move, keep body low and dip at the hips ready to move and elevate.)

PRACTICE 4: FRONT TO JUMP
NUMBERS: THREE

Defender to track and mark attacker's change of direction and then maintain speed to intercept a high pass.

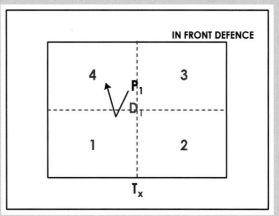

Practice Outcomes

* To track an attacker using good body angles when attacker on a change of direction.

* To use variety of movement patterns to change from a sprint to elevating and intercepting.

* To be ball-side.

* To force ball carrier to pass a high ball.

* To use a one- and two-footed take-off to elevate.

* To execute second-stage marking.

Task/Group Organization

Use a quarter of the court area making sure players work up and down (four coloured flat markers define the area).

Thrower passes to attacker (P), who has to move into two areas before receiving the pass in the second area only.

Coach could call a number for attacker to move into area 1–4.

Attackers complete five to ten repetitions and repeat and change roles.

Progressions and Differentiation

Can add another thrower on other side so ball passed thrower to thrower (wide vision and movement of defender).

Move into three areas before receiving a pass.

Potential Question to Pose

When moving to the spaces what information should you be aware of?

(Answer: Location of attacker and choice of pass, are they quick to change direction, how do they elevate, receive ball?)

PRACTICE: PUSH IN AND OUT
NUMBERS: SEVEN

Defender to mark the space, force players in or wide to gain possession and stop attackers receiving a pass.

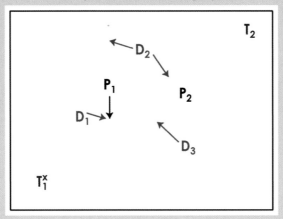

Practice Outcomes

* To track attacker using body angles (first stage) marking on front player nearest ball carrier.

* To stop attackers getting front position.

* To be ball-side and recover quickly to second-stage marking.

* To use body angles and vision to see all defenders.

Task/Group Organization

Use a quarter of the court area, making sure players work up and down.

Thrower passes to attacker (P1 or P2) who has to move to get free from three defenders.

P1 and P2 have to make six to eight passes.

P1 and P2 can use T1 and T2 to pass to but does not count.

Three attempts to achieve six to eight passes.

Progressions and Differentiation

Can add another defender and drip feed in or add defenders together.

Allow throwers to move in limited space.

Ask attackers to keep balls flat and fast.

Potential Question to Pose

What as a team of defenders can you do to limit the options of the attackers?

(Answer: Double team non-ball carrier, angle body to see each other, apply three stages of defence, deny space and force all attackers to middle, sides and so on.)

PRACTICE: FACING IN NUMBERS: EIGHT

Players in threes working together to limit options, be ball-side and deny space.

Practice Outcomes

* To use the three stages of defence to limit attackers' options and movement.

* To position body to face and mark inwards to middle space, protecting the pass to nearest Ts, forcing longer throw.

* To use a quick transition to open up vision to observe all attackers and defenders.

Task/Group Organization

Attackers are moving to a specified target.

Five to ten passes, dependent on fitness levels.

Use a quarter-court area, players work inside the line between throwers.

(Attackers and defenders, no bibs to overload in terms of vision).

Attackers can pass to Ts, but not to count in total number of passes being executed.

Progressions and Differentiation

Throwers can pass to each other.

Add another ball at T3.

Bring Ts closer or further way, or move in and out while practice in action/motion.

Potential Question to Pose

What are the particular strengths of each attacker?

(Answer: Speed, agility, quick change of pace, or height and so on.)

PRACTICE: CUES AND ANGLES
NUMBERS: SIX

Defender must mark first stage defence and keep front position while ball is moved through the area.

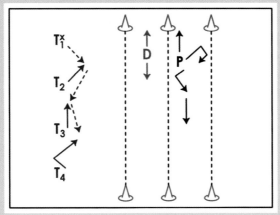

Practice Outcomes

* To keep front position and be able to see ball and attacker, limit head movement.

* To stop attackers being ball-side.

* To use pushing and sliding movement and keep angle, so as to have sight of attacker and ball carrier.

* To intercept or deny passing option.

* To read cues of ball carrier.

Task/Group Organization

Use a half of a third of the court.

Defender must stay in front of designated line between two markers.

P must be attacker behind allocated markers.

Ts must move to receive pass in straight line, with variety of movements passing 1–4 and back again.

Ts can pass to P at any time.

Progressions and Differentiation

Attackers can pass using only flat pass.

Add defence second stage, marking in front of Ts.

Potential Question to Pose

What cues are would signal appropriate time to make an interception?

(Answer: Speed of turn of Ts, speed of release of Ts, movement of P, eyes of ball carrier.)

PRACTICE: SWITCH AND DROP
NUMBERS: FOUR

**Players work in twos to limit options, force an error, deny forward
movement to circle edge and gain interceptions.**

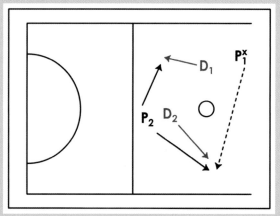

Practice Outcomes

* To move backwards to intercept, force lifted ball or a change of direction by the attacker.

* To position with the body facing inwards to the middle space.

* To force attackers to make an error and gain possession.

Task/Group Organization

Use the centre channel on a half-court.

D1 slightly off-line and moving into space behind (straight line for attacker).

P1 to pass to P2; if pass to P2 on D1 side D1 to attempt intercept.

If pass to P2 on the other side D2 to attempt intercept, D1 and D2 to pick up and track players as they try to get to circle edge. No overhead passes.

Progressions and Differentiation

Add another attacker and defender.

Gain points for limiting options.

No arms over.

Potential Question to Pose

What perceptual cues does the back defender need to have observed?

(Answer: 3-second rule, space and timing of both movers, vision of the front and back defenders, relationship of space for both, when to use arms over, jump on pass.)

PRACTICE: BALL-SIDE NUMBERS: TEN

Defenders have to use movement to be ball-side, while the attackers are penetrating space to the post.

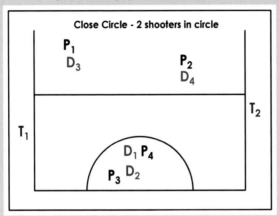

Close Circle - 2 shooters in circle

Practice Outcomes

* To be ball-side using a range of movement skills.

* To angle the body and make the attacker lead away from the straight line.

* To deny forward space and force attackers out and away from the ball carrier.

Progressions and Diffe rentiation

Add another ball starting at T or P.

Add another defender 'floating' in court to take interceptions especially to Ts or any lifted pass.

Gain points for limiting attacking options, for example, non-use of the first mover, attackers have to use Ts, Ts have to pass to each other – or give success points.

Task/Group Organization

P1 or P2 start with ball and ball carrier calls 'ball-side' and holds on to ball until all defenders are ball-side.

P1 and P2 pass to each other at least once or use Ts before passing to shooter. Ball carrier must call 'ball-side', Ts can pass to each other – defenders call 'swing' and get ball-side.

Shooters must stay in the goal circle.

Shooters must pass to each other five to seven times before taking a shot – each ball carrier must keep calling 'ball-side'.

Potential Question to Pose

What might the back defenders do when the front defenders are ball-side?

(Answer: Be ready to come off own attacker to intercept any long or lifted pass, angle body to force attacker in opposite direction away from the straight line.)

PRACTICE: CUT IT OUT
NUMBERS: FIVE

Defenders have to use movements to be ball-side and keep with attacker, who uses a front or back cut, a lead, roll or pivot.

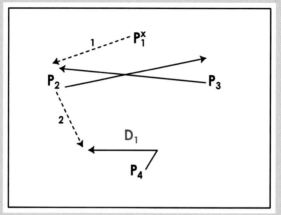

Practice Outcomes

* To be ball-side.

* To execute change of angles and movement to gain possession from attackers.

* To keep high body position and use peripheral vision to sight ball and player.

* To read cues of ball carrier when initiating a pass to attacker.

Task/Group Organization

P1 passes to P2 or P3, who have crossed over and on receipt of ball must turn and pass to P4.

P4 must use front or back cut, lead or roll/pivot to get free from D1.

Attackers must only pass on the straight line and then diagonal if defender in front position. If D successful, passes to P4 and D drops back to mark P1 and P2 and P3 leads across again.

If P4 gets ball, do the same.

Progressions and Differentiation

Make space smaller or larger.

Add defenders on attackers – all at once or drip-feed.

Add two attackers behind D1.

Passers P2 and P3 have to use another pass between them before sighting P4.

Potential Question to Pose

What cues must be read from the ball carriers in order to gain possession?

(Answer: Turn of the hips and shoulders, ball position in relation to body and arms and hands, angle of feet – are they stepping through the pass?)

PRACTICE: WORKING AN AREA
NUMBERS: SIX

One versus one defending, in a specific area, to stay in front and delay, also marking the baseline movement of a shooter.

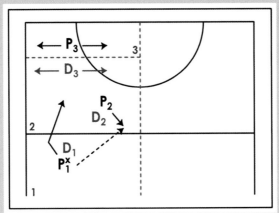

Practice Outcomes

* To force attackers wide and off the circle edge.

* To position body to keep front position.

* To execute arms over with fast transition from first- to second-stage defending.

* To turn towards the ball carrier using a quick turn or roll/pivot.

* To execute stage-three marking.

Task/Group Organization

Use flat markers to highlight baseline movement.

Attackers work ball and must receive two passes in each area 1–3, attempting to pass to shooter in circle who will take a shot.

Defenders delay, one-to-one mark and try to force errors or gain possession using stages of defending.

Progressions and Differentiation

* Allow one catch in each area, or three, or dictate to each person a set number before practice starts.

* Start with throw-in on the sideline or back line for attackers.

* Add another shooter and defender only in goal circle.

Potential Question to Pose

When might it be applicable to get behind the shooter in defence? (Not ball-side.)

(Answer: When close to back line, when stopping a drive to the post.)

PRACTICE: HIDE AND FLY
NUMBERS: FIVE

Defending around the goal circle, where circle and centre court defenders work together to create possession.

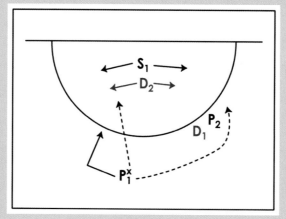

Practice Outcomes

* To execute 'hidden-hand' third-stage defending in order to gain possession.

* To position body to keep high upper body and the front position.

* To read off the ball carrier and other attackers as to line of delivery of the pass.

* To commit to gain an interception.

* Transition from defence to attack – use of quick outlet straight-line double play (give and go).

Task/Group Organization

Use flat markers to highlight half of goal circle.

P1 has choice of passing to shooter or high corner pass to feeder P2.

D1 must keep front position.

P1 can only give hard, flat pass to shooter or high lofted pass to P2.

D2 to have hidden hand at side of body.

D2 must keep front and time movement if ball lifted to P2 into corner.

Use 'give and go' (double play) and take to centre third if intercept.

Progressions and Differentiation

Add another shooter and defender in circle.

Add another attacker and feeder at other side of circle

Add defender on P1.

Potential Question to Pose

What are the strengths of each of the defenders – could the centre court take the high ball?

(Answer: To have a discussion about strengths.)

PRACTICE: DEEP TRAP
NUMBERS: SEVEN

Defending an area and reducing space available.

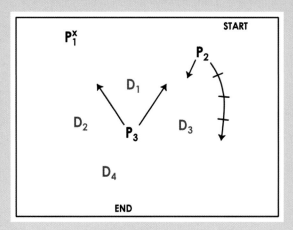

Practice Outcomes

* To stop penetration of space by using zoning as a defensive strategy.

* To slow down a team with fast passing and movement tempo.

* To place pressure on the ball carrier.

* To identify strengths and weaknesses of each defender.

* To devise strategies' to outwit opponents and pressure them to make errors.

* To drop off ball carrier and front-mark straight-line mover.

Task/Group Organization

Use flat markers to highlight a half of a third area.

Attackers to make a minimum of six to eight passes.

Defenders must work to stop the attackers gaining front position. If P1 makes a move to get free in the seam between D1 and D2, then D1 and D2 must make a movement to close this space and force a pass to P2. This is where D3 will come into operation to intercept, or if pass is deeper D4 will intercept.

The defenders can rotate.

Progressions and Differentiation

All defenders to play in different roles.

Add another attacker behind D4.

Make condition so that have to pass within 2 seconds, no faking of pass.

No double plays.

Potential Question to Pose

What are the strengths of each of the defenders?

(Answer: Discussion over strengths, communication of this scenario, vision and calling.)

PRACTICE: TOUGH ON ONE NUMBERS: FIVE

In front defending using a variety of defensive movement skills to close down space and deny an attacker the front position.

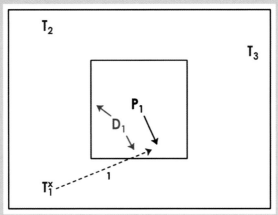

Practice Outcomes

* To stop the attacker getting a front position.

* To react to ball carrier's position and to move while ball in air to limit attacker's options.

* To be ball-side.

* To gain possession or force errors.

* To execute a range of movements in and around attacker in small space (including reverse pivot and turn to take high pass).

Progressions and Differentiation

Ts can move in towards specific area and out again.

Can only use hard, flat pass to P1.

Add defender on Ts and add another defender and attacker in area.

Task/Group Organization

Use flat markers to show area about 5–7m square, work for 30 seconds.

Throwers start with ball and try to pass to P1, who uses a variety of movements to get free.

P1 can go out of specified area, but defender stays in area.

Ts can pass to each other.

Gain points for tips and interceptions, or errors or breaking of rules.

Potential Question to Pose

What are the strengths of the attacker when they are trying to get free in a small space?

(Answer: Discussion about strengths, communication of this and how to combat them.)

PRACTICE: RECOVER AND ARMS OVER NUMBERS: TEN

To track attackers and limit passing options.

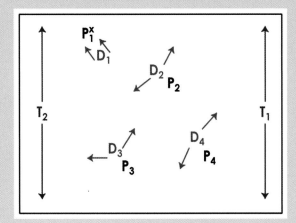

Practice Outcomes

* To use delaying movements to force attackers wide and away from ball carrier – to try to get attackers to move to opposite sides.

* To position body to keep front position, but using wide stance to stop attackers and force another movement to get free.

* To execute arms over with fast transition from first- to second- to third-stage defending.

Task/Group Organization

Work up and down the court area in a half of a third.

Attackers pass ball twice, then must pass to a T nearest them – nearest defender to get arms over T.

Defenders delay, one-to-one mark and try to force errors or gain possession using stages of defending.

Bibs for attackers but not Ts.

Progressions and Differentiation

Allow number of passes to increase before a pass to T.

Ts can pass to each other.

Defenders gain possession and reverse roles after three attempts.

Potential Question to Pose

How might the defence work together to limit the options?

(Answer: Use a call such as 'ball' and be ready to anticipate when a number of passes are used by attackers.)

PRACTICE: TRI-CHALLENGE
NUMBERS: NINE TO FIFTEEN

Defenders apply pressure and deny attacker movement on the straight line.

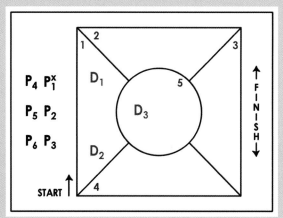

Practice Outcomes

* To angle body to see ball and attacker and other defenders.

* To stop attackers being ball-side.

* To use a sliding movement and have quick recovery step for second-stage defending.

* To intercept or deny a passing option.

* To work as a team to force attackers wide or to middle of space.

Task/Group Organization

Use a half of a third and width of the court.

Two defenders allowed in each space/area at any one time.

Ps attack through the space in threes.

Ps must receive a pass in each area/space.

D starts with ball and passes to a P, then pressures ball carrier at second stage.

Progressions and Differentiation

Attackers move through area without a ball and defenders deny movement – count timing of delay.

Three defenders in each space/area.

Make spaces/area larger or smaller.

Potential Question to Pose

When might a defender move up to a player?

(Answer: To close down the forward space.)

PRACTICE: RISK-READER
NUMBERS: NINE

Players work in threes to deny space, track, limit options and gain possession.

T_1X_1

P_2

D_3

T_2

D_1

T_3

P_1

D_2

X_2T_4

Practice Outcomes

* To use stages of defence to limit attacker options and movement through the space/area.

* To be ball-side and marking a player in their area.

* To read others' intentions and be able to dictate and limit the options of attackers.

* To use broad external vision to intercept.

Task/Group Organization

Use two netballs, start at T1 and T4.

Use a half of a third area.

Ps to pass to each other or use T2/T3.

Coach designates number of passes to be made by Ps or Ds work for 60–120 seconds.

T1 and T4 must constantly pass long throws to each other and Ds to intercept any pass.

Progressions and Differentiation

T2 and T3 to move along area.

T3 and T4 can pass to any T or P.

Potential Question to Pose

What strategies or tactics might the Ds employ?

(Answer: One on-ball carrier and others 1v1, cover front and back space, call ball/space.)

PRACTICE: SLIP, SLIDE SHUFFLE
NUMBERS: NINE TO EIGHTEEN

Defenders to mark the space using slide, shuffle and stop to deny movement.

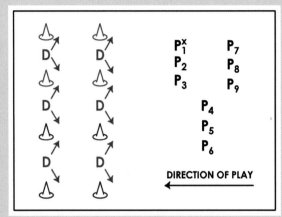

Practice Outcomes

* To track attacker using body angles (first stage) and face marking to restrict.

* To stop attackers getting the front position.

* To be ball-side and attempt intercept.

* To use body angles and vision to see all defenders.

* To use push off outer foot and keep balanced power in stance.

Progressions and Differentiation

Can close down or open up space in front and behind attackers.

Allow throwers to move in limited space or ask attackers to keep balls flat or lifted.

Task/Group Organization

Use a third of the court, using flat markers/lines 3–5m apart, making sure working up and down court.

Ps in 3s to penetrate space – can have two waves of Ps working through area.

Minimum of five passes.

Potential Question to Pose

What are the attackers doing to penetrate the space?

(Answer: Change of direction, sudden stop, front cut, fake pass.)

PRACTICE: THE FLY
NUMBERS: FIVE

Defenders to mark the space in front of attacker and fly for an intercept.

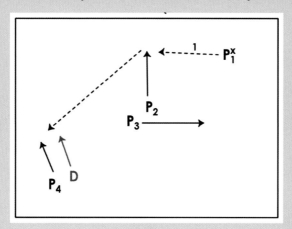

Practice Outcomes

* To be off-line of attacker and attempt the long pass.

* To keep the front position.

* To use body angles and vision to time the intercept in the passing lane.

* To intercept at full stretch.

* Read cues linked to the ball carrier.

Task/Group Organization

Use a half of two-thirds of the court.

P passes to a split lead, choosing P2 or P3.

D must let P4 take the first foot placement.

If D in front and ball-side, P2 and P3 can make another pass and penetrate down other channel.

Progressions and Differentiation

Add defenders to Ps – drip-feed in.

Add another D and P to receive long pass.

Encourage double-dodge of P4.

Potential Question to Pose

What cues would D need to be conscious of when marking P4?

(Answer: Change of direction, speed off the mark, ball carriers turn in the air, release time and point of release, pace of ball.)

PRACTICE: ANTICIPATE AND SWITCH NUMBERS: SIX

Defenders to shadow and be ball-side while first-stage marking and be able to intercept or switch to other players.

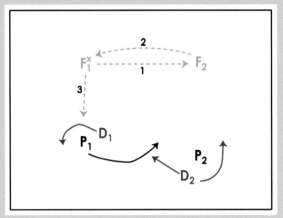

Practice Outcomes

* To move backwards to intercept or force a lifted ball.

* To position body to force attacker to move backwards.

* To deny forwards space and force attackers into middle space.

Task/Group Organization

Feeders to pass continuously to each other and try to pass to Ps.

Defenders to stop straight-line pass and force pass overhead where back defender attempts intercept.

Ds balance and close down the space and switch to other P if needed.

No overhead passes.

Progressions and Differentiation

Add another ball in-between feeders as a loose ball.

Gain points for limiting attacking options, for example 3 seconds, attackers have to double-dodge or change direction.

No arms over.

Potential Question to Pose

What perceptual cues does the back defender need to have observed?

(Answer: 3-second rule, space and timing of both movers, relationship of space for both defenders [strength and weaknesses].)

PRACTICE: FIVE AND IN
NUMBERS: EIGHT

Defenders to mark in the front position and mark the shooter lead outside of the circle.

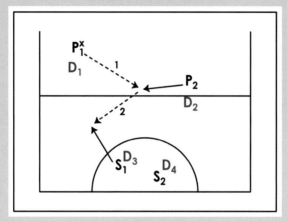

Practice Outcomes

* To recover quickly through all three stages of defence.

* To use quick first-foot plant and sprint to take the interception as the shooter leads out of the circle.

* To use jump or step-back recovery and off-hand to intercept.

Task/Group Organization

Feeders to pass to each other as they attack the circle edge.

To pass to a shooter on a lead outside of the attacking circle.

Defenders stop straight-line pass.

When shooters receive ball in circle they pass out and in five times before taking a shot.

No overhead passes.

Progressions and Differentiation

Feeders to hold ball for 1, 2 or 3 seconds.

Shooters to pass shooter to shooter.

Points for delay of play or force movement of attackers off straight line.

Potential Question to Pose

What can centre-court defenders do to assist the circle defence?

(Answer: Force feeders together, keep them off circle edge, use second-stage defence and use arms to get ball lifted.)

PRACTICE: BACK UP AND GO
NUMBERS: FOUR

Defender to use backwards movement and use a one- or two-footed take-off for a high-ball intercept.

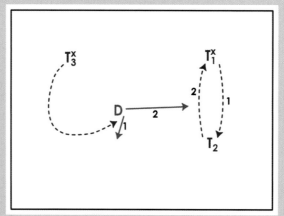

Practice Outcomes

* To execute quick backwards movement and elevation to take a high ball.

* To use timing and body angles to assist peripheral vision, sight and time movement for a fast sprint.

* To make a transition from one movement into another – elevate, land and ready to sprint (reaction).

Task/Group Organization

Throwers 1 and 2 continuously pass a ball to each other.

Thrower 3 throws high pass into space behind defender.

Defender to move backwards and upwards and contest high pass and then anticipate interception between T1 and T2.

Defender pass ball back to T3.

Progressions and Differentiation

T1 and 2 to have a ball each.

Add attacker on D.

Add attacker behind T1 and 2.

Potential Question to Pose

Where in the game situation might these skills be needed?

(Answer: Coming off a tall goal shooter, intercepting outside circle and marking at the centre pass.)

PRACTICE: TOUGH TRIANGLE
NUMBERS: FOUR

Defenders to mark in front position, come off and drive using sprinting and sliding movements around players.

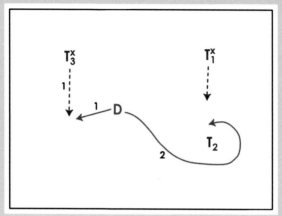

Practice Outcomes

* To mark in front and stop straight-line pass to attacker.

* To use sliding and short foot placement with high body position going around a player with no contact – use off-hand or inside-foot plant and contest throw/pass.

* D to read off the ball placement.

Task/Group Organization

D to sprint and take two-handed pass from T3.

D then sprints and slides around T2 (stationary) and use off-hand or one-handed intercept at full stretch.

Keep throws fast and straight or low.

Variety of passes

Progressions and Differentiation

Add another ball at T2, who places bounce for D to tip.

Add attacker behind D.

T1 and T3 to pass balls to each other.

Add D between T1 and T3.

Potential Question to Pose

What cues must the defender be observing?

(Answer: Ball carriers holding point, release point, body position, speed of release, vision and head position, feet placement.)

PRACTICE: CHALLENGE THE PASSING LANE NUMBERS: FOUR

Defender to read the movements of players on a wide angle and use their vision to sight the ball carrier and strive to intercept in the passing lane.

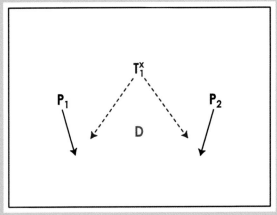

Practice Outcomes

* To read information between ball carrier and attackers (attention).

* To use quick first-foot plant and sprint to take interception either side of the body.

* To be off-line and anticipate the pace of the ball and speed of the movement.

* To use a fast transition and double play.

Task/Group Organization

Thrower to pass ball to self and then to P1 or P2.

Defender to read cues and time movement to challenge for the interception between T and Ps.

If D intercepts then link with T1 and use a double play.

Progressions and Differentiation

Variety of release points of throw from the ball carrier.

Variety of timing and speed of movements from Ps.

Add defender for second-stage defence on T1.

Potential Question to Pose

What areas of the body must the defender cue into (attention and memory retrieval) on the ball carrier and Ps' movement?

(Answer: Eyes, quick or slow release, ball position, body alignment, feet placement.)

PRACTICE: BE AWARE
NUMBERS: EIGHT

A 4v4 working on effective transitions and strategies to use on a turnover.

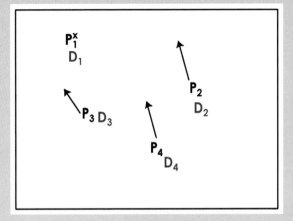

Practice Outcomes

* To improve the reaction of defenders to pick up a loose ball.

* To deny movement to pick up the loose ball.

* To devise a strategy for communication and anticipation between members of the unit.

Task/Group Organization

Ps to pass ball to each other for eight to twelve passes. Ball is thrown or put down and defenders must react quickly and gain possession. Defence then become the attackers.

Could work for 30–60 seconds.

On call or whistle or hand signal from coach ball thrown into space.

Progressions and Differentiation

When ball is 'unclaimed' the attackers could delay.

Coach to count the time taken to gain possession.

Another ball is added.

Potential Question to Pose

What methods of communication or skill do you need to be able to react and have safe and fast transitions?

(Answer: Solve problems by nearest player to ball calling, use a double play with nearest attacker, look for fast break and long pass/outlet.)

PRACTICE: EASY COLOURS NUMBERS: TWO

Defender to use outside foot plant for a change of direction, reacting to a call on court and intercepting two-handed.

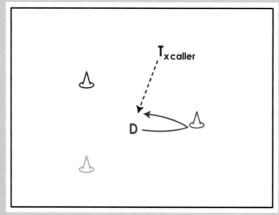

Practice Outcomes

* To recover quickly on change of direction using outside foot placement.

* To use two hands to intercept.

* To use memory and movement and quick reaction.

* To change body angles to see ball and space.

Task/Group Organization

Thrower to call colour and D moves to this colour and T pass ball to middle space.

To use variety of throwing actions.

T calls two colours and then three, D to react and move to all colours before intercepting in middle space.

Encourage two-handed intercept.

No overhead passes.

Progressions and Differentiation

Add one or two feeders and two balls around cones.

To add attacker in middle space.

Make space smaller or larger, narrower or wider.

Potential Question to Pose

Where would these types of movements benefit a defender on court?

(Answer: Marking and tracking an attacker on a straight-line move, coming off an attacker for an intercept.)

PRACTICE: COLOUR AND NUMBER NUMBERS: THREE

Defender to react to number or colour call and working on memory retrieval.

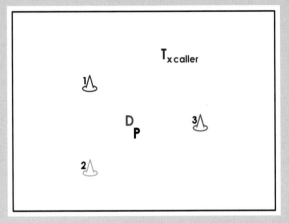

Practice Outcomes

* To keep front position on the attacker.

* To execute stage-one defending and be able to mark a variety of movements.

* To develop the capacity to retrieve information from memory.

Task/Group Organization

T will call numbers or colours.

D will move from centre of space and react to go to selected number or colour.

D is marking in front on P, who will use short leads.

P can move to calls and D must contest any pass to P.

Progressions and Differentiation

P to use variety of movement to include: changes of direction, lunges and double-dodges.

Add another T.

Potential Question to Pose

How does the attacker get free most effectively?

(Answer: Choice of movement that she knows will outwit.)

PRACTICE: TRIPLE CHOICE NUMBERS: TWO

Defender to react to number and colour call, remove and keep brief.

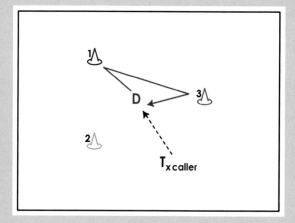

Practice Outcomes

* To retrieve information from memory.

* To react to ball coming into space and change movement pattern.

* To change body angles to sight the ball carriers.

Task/Group Organization

T will call numbers and colours.

D will move from centre of space and react to go to a selected number and /or colour.

D to have body position and vision to see ball and corner/cone.

Pass can be put anywhere in the triangle.

Progressions and Differentiation

T can move outside the area after each pass to a defender.

Add Ts.

Add another ball two balls and three Ts.

Potential Question to Pose

Where would a player have difficulty sighting both ball and space/cone?

(Answer: When on a change of direction or when the head drops.)

PRACTICE: BRING IT ON
NUMBERS: FOUR

Defenders to mark on the front to execute movement around a marker and strive to intercept.

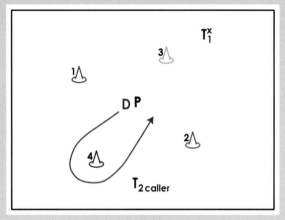

Practice Outcomes

* To retrieve information quickly from memory when the call is made.

* To react to ball and player when moving around a cone.

* To take intercept at full stretch.

Task/Group Organization

T will call numbers or colours.

D will move around the cone.

D to have body position and vision to see ball and P.

T1 can pass to T2 or P when D is coming off cone.

D can intercept pass between Ts.

Progressions and Differentiation

Feeders to hold ball for 1, 2 or 3 seconds.

Add another D in middle.

Have more Ts and Ds on outside area and moving.

Potential Question to Pose

What are the strengths of the defender?

(Answer: They are dependent upon physical attributes and focus of attention.)

PRACTICE: BRAIN BOX
NUMBERS: FOUR

Defender to mark on the front position to limit movement of the attacker.

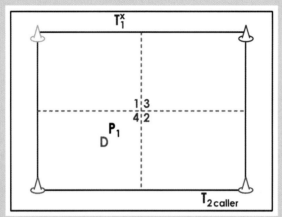

Practice Outcomes

*   To use memory retrieval and movement selection when listening to a call.

*   To react to ball and player when moving around a cone.

*   To take an intercept at full stretch.

*   To use all three stages of defence.

Task/Group Organization

T1 with ball, T2 call number for space or colours of cone.

P has to move to this area and D keeps front position.

T can pass when P is deemed to be free.

Progressions and Differentiation

Change call to top, base, left or right.

Add another D in middle.

Have more Ts and Ds on the outside area and moving.

Add another ball.

Potential Question to Pose

What actions can the defender do if the attacker P gets the ball?

(Answer: Arms over on second-stage defence, try to drop on to the T to intercept, recover to a denial position to force into side or out of area/space.)

CHAPTER 6

PRACTICES THAT INTEGRATE PSYCHOLOGICAL SKILLS

Mental skills are often neglected within sports training generally, being left to develop while the focus is on the physical, technical or tactical elements. There are many techniques available to enhance confidence, control, commitment and concentration, but as netball is a team sport communication skills also need consideration. This chapter aims to emphasize the mental skills within practices to encourage the development of a positive mindset and the ability to control those thought processes.

Goal-Setting

Goal-setting is one of the most versatile mental skills and identifies personal targets that increase commitment and effort levels. Tracking of goals builds confidence and sustains motivation in the long term. Goals used within a practice setting provide a very clear guide as to what players should be concentrating on at that particular time. The more specific the goals, the easier it is to see whether they have been achieved or not, so some way of measuring them helps and a time-scale for achieving the goals is a useful guide for the player. Goals work best when they are realistic and where an element of flexibility is used to evaluate the goals and adjust them where necessary.

Coaches can use a range of goal types. Goals relating to the outcome of a match can motivate players; however, these are only partially under their control. So it is helpful to underpin these with performance and process goals, which are more under players' control. Performance goals identify a measurable target such as shooting percentages, percentage accuracy of feeds, or times to complete performance elements. They are effective in working towards achieving the outcome goals and are usually more effective when combined with process goals.

Process goals underpin both performance and outcome goals and help the player to focus on specific elements of training or match play, rather than being overtly concerned with the outcome. Process goals encourage task-related thinking, which may be executing a specific coaching point, or using a specific movement or strategy. Process goals are often made more powerful if coupled with a keyword or positive statement that the performer can say to themselves to simulate the type of movement or skill they are about to execute and therefore increase the chance of success.

Goal-setting can be even more effective when players agree the goals with the coach, thereby increasing communication and working across different levels. Agreeing team goals helps motivation and effort at a team level and these can then be broken down into unit goals so that each area of the court has something specific to aim to achieve. Players then identify their specific role within that unit goal. This is known as PRIDE:

* **P**ersonal
* **R**esponsibility
* **I**n
* **D**elivering
* **E**xcellence.

In this way, goal-setting for the individual has context with both the unit work and the team goals. Players can therefore be successful in some elements, even when the overall result may not have gone as expected. Reflections at the end of a session or match can happen on a number of levels and over time this can help to stabilize confidence and manage emotional fall-out when coaches have to make difficult substitution and selection choices.

Concentration Skills

Concentration skills train players to focus on specific cues within the competitive environment and as such

The shooter is confident and in control.

need to be practised within the training environment too. Focusing on appropriate cues and being able to switch attention effectively from one thing to the next needs practice. Players are encouraged to be aware of different focus points and to explore their use in practices. At times, it is appropriate for a player to be concentrating on a specific focal point, usually referred to as a narrow focus of attention. This could involve concentrating on fast feet or extending the arm in preparation for shooting (an internal, narrow focus), or tracking the flight path of the ball to take an early interception (external, narrow focus).

But players also need to practise reading the game to help with their decision-making and this is where practice at the broader end of the spectrum is helpful. Again, this can be taking in information externally, or analysing that information internally. Planning strategy is helpful here, as is reading and interpreting others' strategy and team play. Practising across the range of foci prepares players to cope with distractions, either by shutting them out, or by switching concentration to recover more quickly if their concentration is broken.

Keywords

Keywords or positively phrased short statements can act as triggers to aid concentration and players are asked here to cue into visual and auditory cues to help reduce incidences of breaking the line at a centre pass (hold–whistle–go), as well as responding to a variety of stimuli to help increase visual perception skills.

Imagery

Imagery is where an individual recreates an experience in their mind using information from their senses. Using sights, sounds, emotional responses and feelings of movements makes the image more vivid and can improve confidence, help practise a move, learn a strategy, or be part of a performance routine. As such, imagery can help to control emotions and keep players mentally practising while they are injured. Players may prefer to use imagery by doing the movement in their mind (an internal perspective), which can help in practising specific skills. It encourages players to feel the

Excellent use of body position within one-on-one defence to assist concentration on a breadth of information.

movements as they would be when performed physically and to get in touch with the sights and sounds associated with performing a movement well. Players might do this in pictures, thoughts or feelings, whichever works best for the individual. Or some performers may find it easier to see themselves performing a skill as if they were watching themselves on the television (external perspective). This can really help in strategy development and correcting errors.

Developing Self-Confidence

Developing self-confidence as an individual and as a team can be a good buffer to helping to cope with competitive stress and anxiety and maintaining enjoyment of netball when training gets tough. It will also help players to develop a desire to succeed rather than a fear of failure, which will help them to bounce back from mistakes and be brave enough on court to try new skills and go for interceptions. Building up a bank of previous success is the main way that self-confidence can be developed, so a step-wise approach to the use of goal-setting is powerful here. But self-confidence can also be gained from watching others succeed, by visualizing a good performance and using positive keywords for encouragement. It is also worth working on the image portrayed to others, particularly the opposition, therefore practices that ask players to adopt a mindset of 'strong' or 'it's mine' are helpful in developing assertiveness and 'walking tall' in order to exude an aura of confidence.

Pre-Performance Routines

Pre-performance routines bring all the mental skills together and enable players to adapt their responses to the dynamics of the game when under pressure. Normally routines have stages to help control emotions and refocus the players on a productive mindset. Typically, a routine would start with an emotional outlet to park thoughts of past events or outside influences, possibly with some relaxation to control any tension, and could involve a physical movement to symbolize this, for example, standing up from the bench when preparing to substitute or setting a good, balanced base when looking to shoot. Often players image the response they are aiming to perform and couple this with a keyword to simulate how they will execute the movement before doing so.

These routines need to be variable in length to suit the needs of the player within the game. Longer versions can be useful to prepare players before a match, after a break or when being substituted. Shorter versions can be used to manage emotions in response to distractions, opposition antics ('sledging') or umpiring decisions that do not go as expected. Practicing routines can improve consistency and confidence in setting up to shoot, recovering from mistakes or can open up vision before taking a centre pass.

The following practices include a variety of ideas where these mental skills can be made more overt and applied to game scenarios to help develop greater mental toughness in players.

PRACTICE: USE KEYWORDS
NUMBERS: FOUR

Players are asked to identify keywords to focus their efforts on improving specific elements of a change of direction.

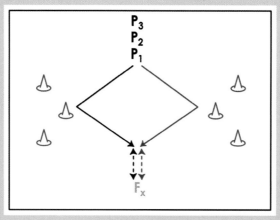

Practice Outcomes

* To explore different keywords to find which one will help improve performance most.

* To improve performance of a change of direction and receive a hard, straight pass.

* To choose the element of the change of direction on which to focus.

Progressions and Differentiation

Explore different keywords to find the most effective.

Develop keywords for different elements of the movement.

Vary positioning of cones, angle of run.

Apply to specific areas of the court.

Add defence.

Task/Group Organization

Work down court in any area.

P1 chooses cone to execute change of direction to receive straight ball from F

P2 visits a different cone from P1; P3 visits a different cone from P2.

Repeat five times continuously.

Players review change of direction.

Choose a specific focus to improve.

Identify keyword to help simulate the movement to be executed.

Repeat using the keyword – in head or out loud.

Potential Question to Pose

What keyword helps in focusing thoughts and efforts?

(Answer: For example, 'plant', 'drive' for sharpness; 'go', 'drive', 'pump arms' to drive out of turn to ball.)

PRACTICE: SET SOME GOALS
NUMBERS: SIX

Players are challenged to use different goals to improve performance of movement skills.

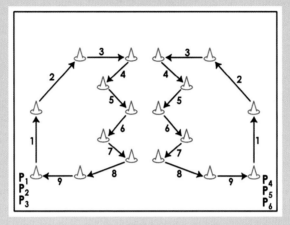

Practice Outcomes

* To choose a specific element of performance and use a keyword to focus efforts (a 'process goal').

* To identify a measurable performance goal for which to aim, for example, time to complete a circuit.

* To choose whether to aim for an outcome goal or not, for example, compete against others.

* To understand the impact of different goal types on effort and performance.

Progressions and Differentiation

Include option for outcome goal, for example, compete against others, compare scores.

Swap sides.

Vary position of cones and movement skills included.

Task/Group Organization

Two sets of cones; three players at each start point.

P1 sprints, changes direction at 2, sidesteps at 3, sprints 4–7, crossover steps at 8. Complete two repetitions.

Set own process goal and keyword.

Repeat – review – repeat.

Set performance goal.

Repeat two repetitions.

Potential Question to Pose

What effect did each type of goal have?

(Answer: Process – focus on specific element; Performance – scores/time, can see improvement; Outcome – beat others.)

PRACTICE: PROCESS GOALS IN CIRCLE DEFENCE
NUMBERS: FIVE

Players are challenged to improve their performance of 'boxing out' in defence with the use of specific process goals.

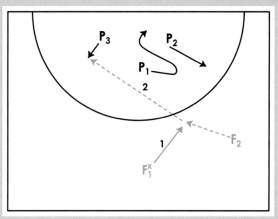

Practice Outcomes

* To use process goals to help the circle defence to drive for an intercept, recover quickly to box out incoming shooter and take the rebound.

* To decide on focus point to improve performance.

* To use keywords to help.

* To develop strength of boxing out.

* To develop speed of transition between different defensive skills.

Progressions and Differentiation

Feeders give pass to P2 if P1 not committed to intercept enough.

Vary positioning and movement of shooters and defence.

Task/Group Organization

F1 feeds ball to F2 as they drive to the circle edge.

P2 moves to receive ball from F2.

P1 drives out for the intercept.

F2 fakes pass and gives ball to P3, who shoots.

P1 recovers quickly to box out P2 and take the rebound.

Five repetitions.

Player decides which element of performance to focus on in the next five repetitions. Use keyword(s) to help.

Repeat and run twice through.

Potential Question to Pose

Which element to focus on? Which keyword will help?

(Answer: Varied, but check for specific focus. Keywords could include 'drive/go', 'turn', 'back to shooter', 'strong', 'up'.)

PRACTICE: COMBINE YOUR GOALS
NUMBERS: EIGHT

Players will identify and use both performance and process goals while driving to the circle edge to feed shooters.

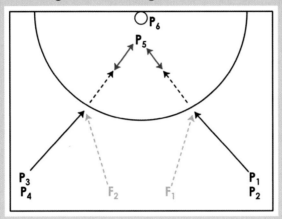

Practice Outcomes

* To identify performance goals to monitor player improvement.

* To identify and use process goals to underpin the achievement of the performance goal(s).

* To develop confidence in the execution of:

  – driving to the circle edge to receive a feed;

  – body management to control momentum and stay onside;

  – delivering good feeds to the shooters.

Task/Group Organization

P1 drives to the circle edge to receive feed from F2, controls momentum and feeds P5, who turns and shoots.

P6 collects rebounds and returns ball safely.

As P5 shoots, P3 drives to circle edge to receive feed from F2, feeds P5, who turns and shoots.

Five repetitions.

Players identify specific performance goal and underpinning process goals.

Repeat five repetitions.

Review goals, redefine if necessary and repeat.

Progressions and Differentiation

Change sides.

Vary feed and angles of run.

Include P6 as second shooter.

Add defence.

Potential Questions to Pose

What performance goal could be used?

(Answer: Varied, for example, success in receiving, staying onside or feeding.)

What process goals could help?

(Answer: Drive on to circle edge, bend knees, hold, soften before feed.)

PRACTICE: PLAY WITH PRIDE
NUMBERS: SIX

Players are asked to identify their 'Personal Responsibility In Delivering Excellence' (PRIDE), within a defensive/attacking unit.

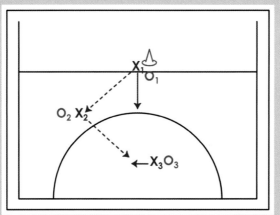

Practice Outcomes

* To identify a specific focus as a unit goal within a modified game, for example, use of all three channels in attack, angle run for ball, get ball-side; tight one-on-one, use of body position as a team to deny space.

* To identify and share each individual's contribution to that unit goal (PRIDE), for example, clear communication, positive drive on to ball.

* To use the PRIDE goal for players to reflect back on their individual success, as well as the unit success.

Task/Group Organization

Identify unit focus for attack and defence. Share individual goals.

3v3 in a third of the court.

Game starts on the third line, only two players can go in the circle, otherwise players move freely.

When a goal is scored, start again at the cone, non-scoring team takes the pass in.

Continuous play for 4 minutes.

Review and adapt goals – refine PRIDE.

Repeat – review own performance, whether PRIDE was achieved or not.

Progressions and Differentiation

Progress to half-court game with specific unit strategies, giving the PRIDE more game context.

Use in pre-match preparation and post-match review.

Potential Question to Pose

How can an individual contribute to the achievement of their team's goal?

(Answer: Check for specificity and that player is in control, for example angle run to pass, clear out to make space, use of stage three defensive skills.)

PRACTICE: CONCENTRATE! NUMBERS: TWO

A player is introduced to an internal and an external focus of attention while executing single and double leads.

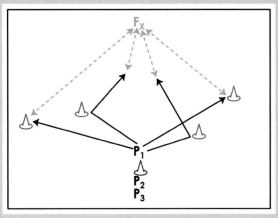

Practice Outcomes

* To understand the use of both an internal and an external focus of concentration to improve performance.

* To identify different examples of internal and external focus to support the development of single and double leads.

* To practise receiving the ball on each side of the body using single and double leads and to receive a hard, fast pass.

Progressions and Differentiation

Players choose which focus.

Increase pace, height and speed of release.

Adapt to position-specific examples.

Task/Group Organization

Position practice anywhere on the court.

P1 drives to cone to receive pass using a single lead (outside cones) and a double lead (inner cones); return to central cone each time.

Three repetitions for warm-up.

Identify coaching point relating to internal focus; use keyword to help.

Three repetitions.

Identify an external point on which to concentrate. Repeat.

Potential Question to Pose

What internal and external focus might help?

(Answer: Internal – 'fast feet', 'drive'; external – 'take ball early in flight path'.)

PRACTICE: USE 'TRIGGERS'
NUMBERS: SEVEN

Players are challenged to identify and use verbal, visual and auditory cues to assist in the use of a change of pace at the centre pass.

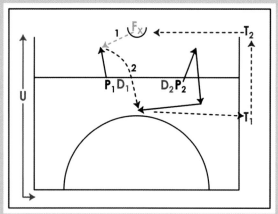

Practice Outcomes

* To use a change of pace at the centre pass for phase one and phase two passes.

* To judge the timing and execution of this change of pace to remain onside and yet get a fast start at the whistle.

* To identify and use triggers – verbal, visual or auditory cues to time moves well.

Progressions and Differentiation

Increase speed of recovery.

Increase percentage effort of defence.

Vary set up and triggers used for phase one and two passes.

Task/Group Organization

P1 and P2 set up at the centre line to use a change of pace to receive the centre pass.

Whistle to simulate timing of centre pass, F delivers pass.

If P1 receives pass, P2 doubles back to receive phase two pass.

T retrieves ball(s) and returns to F to keep intensity.

Five repetitions.

Decide on triggers/keywords to help cue in timing of moves – auditory, visual or verbal.

Repeat five times, using triggers.

Defences work at 60 per cent.

Potential Question to Pose

Which triggers help in timing a move well?

(Answer: 'Hold–whistle–go', 'ready–drive', 'hover–go'.)

PRACTICE: READ THE GAME
NUMBERS: SEVEN

Players practise their broader focus of concentration to improve their reading of the game.

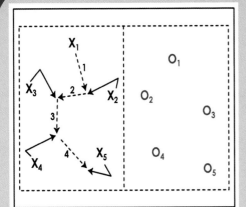 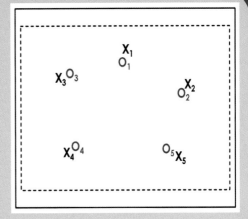

Practice Outcomes

* To plan and agree a sequence of passing within the given area (broad, internal focus).

* To agree a specific focus for that pattern of play (for example, angle of run on to ball).

* To pick up on the opposition's pattern of play while defending them (broad, external focus).

* To report back on patterns of play and check for accuracy.

Task/Group Organization

Two teams of five working.

(a) Each team plans a pattern of play – sequence of passing and movement on and off the ball, with an agreed specific focus, for example, use of roll dodge/change of direction. Practise pattern of play.

(b) Play against other team – 60 per cent defence, run through pattern three times.

Defending team reports back on attacking team's play and focus.

Progressions and Differentiation

Adapt to specific games strategy/tactic.

Agree and plan strategies for match play.

Observe and analyse opposition play.

Potential Question to Pose

How can a player notice what the opposition is doing?

(Answer: Open up vision, look for positioning and movement of team.)

PRACTICE: CONCENTRATE – ON WHAT? WHEN?
NUMBERS: FIVE

Players are required to switch their attention from broad to narrow and from player to ball to improve concentration skills.

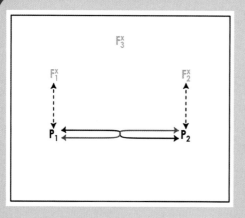 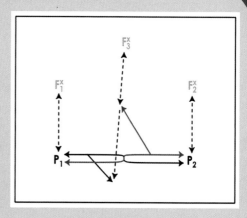

Practice Outcomes

* To encourage players to switch their attention from player to ball and back.

* To encourage players to switch from a narrow to a broader focus of attention and back.

* To maintain effective communication between all players.

Progressions and Differentiation

Increase pace of movement and speed of release.

Return ball to other feeder.

Adapt to court area and add defender.

Task/Group Organization

F1 and F2 each feed hard, straight pass to arrive in the space for P1 and P2 to run on to.

P1 and P2 receive pass and return to feeder received from. Switch places, by moving around each other, before receiving next pass.

Complete six to eight repetitions.

F3 drops in third ball randomly (b). Nearest player moves to pick up the loose ball as fast as possible. Other player drives down court to receive hard, straight pass, returns ball to F3; P1 and 2 resume practice.

Potential Question to Pose

What is the focus of attention at each stage of the practice?

(Answer: Ball, switch to player, back to ball. Notice partner position when loose ball released and respond.)

PRACTICE: SWITCH FOCUS IN ONE-ON-ONE DEFENCE
NUMBERS: FOUR

A player is required to switch their focus of attention while utilizing stage one and two defending skills.

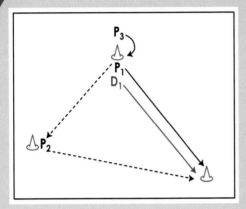
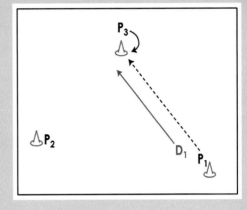

Practice Outcomes

* To switch attention from stage one to stage two defending skills and back.

* To identify which element of switching is most challenging.

* To use keywords/triggers and imagery to improve performance.

Progressions and Differentiation

Increase speed of ball movement.

Vary positioning of cones and keywords used.

Adapt to court-specific work.

Task/Group Organization

P1 passes to P2 (a).

D1 defends P1 using stage-two skills, then switches to stage one as P1 runs to the empty cone to receive the ball from P2. D1 attempts to gain the intercept.

If unsuccessful, D1 defends pass to P4, then recovers (b) to defend P4 as practice sets up again.

D1 remains defender for three rotations.

Identify most challenging element of attention-switching. Visualize how player would like to react, choose keyword to help trigger response. Repeat to try key word.

Potential Question to Pose

How can a player switch effectively from stage two to stage one defending skills?

(Answer: Use of reverse pivot to move from 'hold' to 'fast feet', then 'ball'. Keep head up and open vision.)

PRACTICE: GOAL ATTACK LOOK DOWN!
NUMBERS: FOUR

The player is challenged to open up their vision and look for the direct line pass into the shooter before releasing the ball.

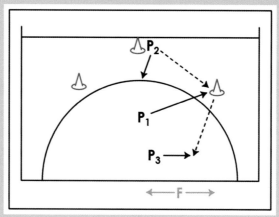

Practice Outcomes

* To practise turning in the air to assist early vision down court.

* To encourage player to turn head early, look for cue down court before releasing the ball.

* To vary angle of drive and turn.

* To vary positioning of P3.

Progressions and Differentiation

Vary position, pace and difficulty to challenge body management of player.

Use both sides of post.

Increase speed of recovery and reset.

Task/Group Organization

P1 drives out of circle to receive pass from P2.

P1 turns to look down court for F, who holds up a coloured cone. P1 calls colour of cone before releasing the ball to P3, who turns and shoots.

P2 moves after releasing the ball to provide option of square pass, if needed.

F varies positioning along backline and colour of cone held up.

P1 rebounds, passes back to P2 to restart from different position.

Six to eight repetitions.

Potential Question to Pose

How can a player turn effectively to be able to see the visual cue down-court?

(Answer: Turn head, look up and forward to encourage vision down-court.)

PRACTICE: RECOGNIZE–RESPOND–RETURN NUMBERS: FIVE

Players are challenged to use positive keywords to increase their speed of response within unit rotational work.

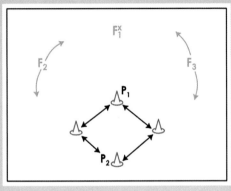 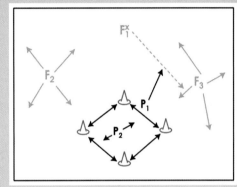

Practice Outcomes

* To use R–R–R as keywords to:

    – recognize the cue card;

    – respond with driving run, as appropriate;

    – return to pattern of movement quickly.

* To move effectively as a unit to cover the space and balance each other.

* To communicate the decision to take the ball effectively.

Progressions and Differentiation

F1 and F2 become mobile, passing between each other to vary feed, F3 shows cue cards.

Lose the call and communicate non-verbally.

Adapt to court areas – shooting rotation, or diamond defence (add 2 × P).

Task/Group Organization

F1 with ball as focal point for P1 and P2.

P1 and P2 work together to move within a diamond shape to cover space and balance each other's movements.

F2 and F3 move around players with coloured cards hidden, one player holds card up.

If green – nearest P calls 'mine' and drives out towards signal and receives pass from F1. Other P balances the cover of space until partner can return.

If red – no response.

F2 and F3 vary position and colour of card.

P1 and P2 use 'recognize–respond–return' to increase speed of response.

Potential Question to Pose

How can a player recognise, respond and return quickly to the cue presented?

(Answer: Keep focus on ball, use body position to keep vision wide to see cue, call and drive hard, recover quickly and adapt to partner.)

PRACTICE: USE IMAGERY – INTERNAL FIRST
NUMBERS: THREE

Players develop their use of internal imagery skills within stage-one defensive skills.

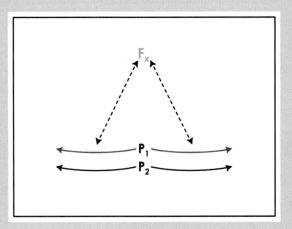

Practice Outcomes

* To practise imaging by 'doing the movement' (internal imagery).

* To increase vividness of the image by using more senses.

* To refresh the image with physical practice.

* To use imagery to improve performance.

* To identify 'best performance' and use to practise the skill mentally.

Task/Group Organization

P2 attempts to get free to receive pass from F within playing area.

F tosses ball to self, catches and looks to feed P2 – to help timing.

P1 adopts stage-one defence skills to stay with P2 and look for intercept.

P1 visualizes what they want to perform, how it will feel, then does it. Four repetitions.

Repeat each imagery four times, then add another sense. Notice the best one.

Progressions and Differentiation

Vary stance to deny the attacker different spaces.

Vary size of area.

Relive good performance with imagery, then practice best performance imagery four times before next training session.

Potential Question to Pose

Describe an image as fully as possible

(Answer will vary but check for positive outcome, the range of senses and encourage reliving the close marking as well as the taking of the intercept.)

PRACTICE: USE IMAGERY – EXTERNAL TOO!
NUMBERS: EIGHT

Players are asked to develop external imagery skills while executing diamond defensive formation at the centre pass.

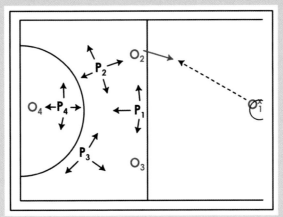

Practice Outcomes

* To use a team defensive strategy to develop external imagery skills.

* To visualize working within a defensive strategy as if watching oneself on TV (external imagery).

* To use imagery to identify and improve difficulties in executing the defensive strategy.

Progressions and Differentiation

Vary positioning of attacking players.

Watch others and use this information to update image.

Use video to enhance accuracy of image.

Task/Group Organization

P1–P4 adopt diamond zone at centre pass, to challenge phase two or three passes.

Take four centre passes.

Players visualize themselves and team executing effective zone. Think through movements as play switches sides, players respond to each other to cover space and go for the intercept. See the team working effectively and the successful challenge for the intercept.

Take four more centre passes.

Discuss images and movements to identify areas of difficulty and visualize desired response.

Take four more centre passes, review and develop.

Potential Question to Pose

How can these imagery skills help in improving performance?

(Answer: Practise skills and tactics in the mind, discuss with others and visualize to improve.)

PRACTICE: COMBINE THE IMAGES
NUMBERS: THREE

Players use practice of a roll dodge to combine imagery types.

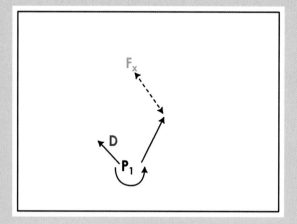

Practice Outcomes

* To use and understand the benefits of internal and external imagery skills to support technical practice.

* To use demonstrations or footage of 'experts' or 'performers' to help to develop external imagery skills.

* To use reflections on the feelings, sights and sounds of executing the roll dodge to develop internal imagery skills.

Task/Group Organization

P1 watches demonstration or video footage of roll dodge a number of times. P1 runs through in their mind the skill, then tries the skill. Step one way to commit D, then pivot to make quick turn around D to receive ball from F. Repeat six times.

Repeat, increase use of senses in image. Relive good dodges before next turn.

Review difficulties, image desired response, use keyword to help. Repeat.

Progressions and Differentiation

Vary side-roll dodge executed. Increase pace, decrease space.

Practise imaging 2–3 minutes a day over four days, sometimes doing the movement, sometimes watching yourself.

Potential Question to Pose

Talk through the image.

(Answer: Varied, but check image is positive/successful, check number of senses used and whether performers can use each type of imagery.)

PRACTICE: CONFIDENT SHOOTERS I – USE A ROUTINE
NUMBERS: THREE

A shooter is asked to develop a pre-shot routine to increase confidence and consistency in the shot.

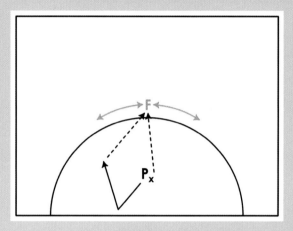

Practice Outcomes

* To develop a secure pre-shot routine that can be sustained under pressure.

* To develop consistency in shot set-up by:

    – use of keywords to 'set up' to shoot;

    – identify specific focus point early and latch on to it;

    – to use breath control to control tension;

    – to use keyword or image to finish shot off.

* To relive successful shots to improve ability to feel the movement.

Task/Group Organization

P starts where most comfortable, shoots from different spot each time, rebounds, then passes to F. P then cuts out and back to receive feed, turns, sets up and shoots. Rebound and repeat five times.

P uses keywords to support stages of set-up and release, for example, to balance, focus, breathe and release to follow through.

Five shots, then on next good one, pause and relive the shot in mind before returning to practise. Review stages of routine, develop intensity of control and repeat.

Progressions and Differentiation

Vary the position of shots and feeds.

Increase speed and difficulty of feed, or number of passes before shooting

Include defence on shot.

Potential Question to Pose

Which keywords help most at different stages of the shot preparation?

(Answer: For example, 'balance', 'set', 'breathe', 'focus', 'tall', 'lift', 'swish', 'fingers'.)

PRACTICE: CONFIDENT SHOOTERS 2 – COPE WITH DISTRACTIONS
NUMBERS: SEVEN

Players are challenged to maintain accuracy whilst being distracted.

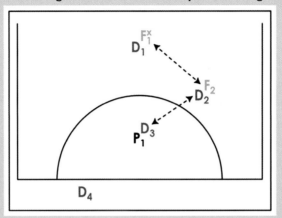

Practice Outcomes

* To be confident in ability to cope with distractions when shooting.

* To use goal-setting and agree distraction and coping strategy.

* To use keywords to help control concentration.

* To maintain emotional control under pressure of distractions.

* To use a range of distractions.

Progressions and Differentiation

Vary distraction given to shooter.

P uses other options – pass and step to shoot to support coping strategies.

Add D4 to increase pressure on P.

Task/Group Organization

3v3 from third line – F1, F2 and P work the ball into a good shooting position. F1 and F2 play as centre/WA, wing attack and goal attack.

Five repetitions, then P agrees the type of distraction to practise against. D3 provides that distraction, for example, D3 defends within 0.9m or knocks P's arm as shoots; or D2 drops back to double-mark P.

P aims to raise awareness of their own response to the repeated use of distraction, uses pre-shot routine and keywords to help focus concentration. Repeat ×10.

P also uses breath control to help relaxation and visualizing good response to improve confidence. Repeat ×10.

Potential Question to Pose

How can focus on a good shot be maintained when being distracted?

(Answer: Use pre-shot routine and keywords to focus on shot, not distraction and breath control to relax shoulders.)

PRACTICE: MENTALLY TOUGH SHOOTERS
NUMBERS: THREE

Players use imagery and keywords to recover from a missed shot.

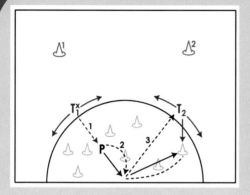 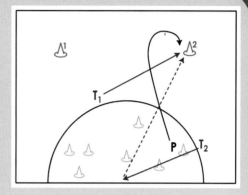

Practice Outcomes

* To enable the shooter to practise replacing the 'missed shot' mindset with a positive image and use of helpful keywords before shooting again.

* To encourage use of imagery and keywords prior to shooting to help accuracy.

* To vary shooting position.

* To respond to a missed shot to simulate a turnaround.

Task/Group Organization

Cones spread randomly in circle with two outlaying cones for 'turnaround'.

T1 feeds P, who shoots, rebounds, passes out to T2 and moves to a different cone for return (a).

If P misses, nearest T collects rebound and looks to feed outlet pass to the other T, who drives to an outlaying cone (b). P recovers up court to use second-stage defence skills against T at the cone, holds for 3 seconds. Then reset.

As P jogs back to reset, focus on regaining positive image and mindset by thinking and feeling desired shot and using positive keyword. When ready, restart practice.

Progressions and Differentiation

Decrease time given to P before restarting.

Once P has arrived at outlaying cone, T1 and T2 can pass between each other so that P recovers mindset during play.

Potential Question to Pose

What can you focus on whilst recovering to help a positive mind set before your next shot?

(Answer: For example, feelings of 'good shot', 'swish', 'smooth', 'steady' will be very individual.)

PRACTICE: CONFIDENT INTERCEPTIONS
NUMBERS: TWO TO FOUR

Players use keywords and concentration skills to improve confidence in taking interceptions.

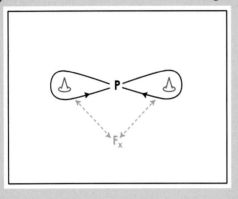 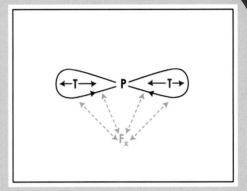

Practice Outcomes

* To use an internal focus of concentration to improve movement skills (for example, fast feet, turn hips).

* To use an external focus to take interception (for example, take ball early)

* To identify early cues to look for intercept.

* To use imagery of intended movement and good interceptions to help to develop confidence.

Progressions and Differentiation

Vary the elements of performance visualized and keywords used, vary direction of movement around cones.

Increase pace and difficulty of feed, allow restricted movement of T.

Contextualize on court.

Task/Group Organization

Two cones approx. 4m apart.

P moves in a figure of 8 around cones, with eyes focused on ball at all times. F feeds ball at any time when P has worked around the cone and can drive forward on to interception.

P visualizes desired movement and drive for interception.

F feeds ball to ensure success at first, for eight repetitions.

P chooses keyword to focus on movement, images and repeats × 8. Then chooses external focus, visualizes and repeats.

At end of set, visualize best performance.

Potential Question to Pose

Which keywords could help in moving quickly? Taking the ball well?

(Answer: 'fast feet', 'turn hips', 'drive', 'take ball early', 'angle drive'.)

PRACTICE: INTERCEPTS – WHEN TO FLY? NUMBERS: THREE

A player improves their confidence and judgment of intercepts from a variety of positions.

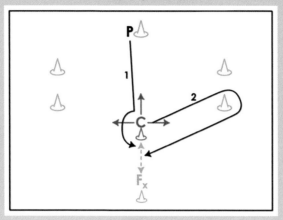

Practice Outcomes

* To develop confidence in choosing when to fly for an interception.

* To develop confidence in taking interceptions form a variety of positions.

* To use imagery to relive good performances.

* To increase confidence in the timings of interceptions.

Task/Group Organization

F floats high feed to C. P starts at first cone, times run to take intercept, returns ball to F.

Reset to next cone and repeat, until all cones completed.

Relive good intercept, choose keyword to help simulate movement and use to support interceptions from other cones.

F and C pass ball. P chooses when to time intercept.

Progressions and Differentiation

Practise the intercept P finds most challenging.

Vary position and distance of cones, increase pace and add restricted movement of C.

Contextualize on court.

Potential Question to Pose

Which cues help in knowing when to go for the interception?

(Answer: Shoulder/arm movement of thrower then flight path of ball, relative position of players.)

PRACTICE: SHOOTERS – ASSERT YOURSELVES!
NUMBERS: SEVEN

Players are challenged to maintain their assertiveness of movement and effectiveness of rotation work under increasing defensive pressure.

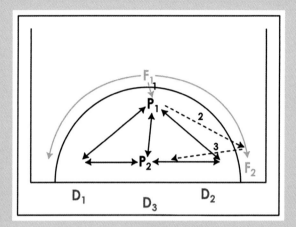

Practice Outcomes

* To maintain quality of movement with increasing pressure of defence.

* To use keywords to assist decisiveness and maintain assertiveness of movement.

* To use triangular rotation to create and use space in the circle effectively.

Progressions and Differentiation

Add D1, then D2 to simulate game.

Start from third line, shooters move freely in and out of circle.

Task/Group Organization

F1 and F2 offer–move–reoffer around the circle edge, maintain passing and looking to feed the circle.

P1 and P2 use triangular rotation to offer potential passing and shooting options. Communicate via non-verbal means to indicate where and when ball is wanted.

Six passes in and out of the circle, then take shot on next good shooting option. Rebound, pass out and restart.

Review, identify opportunities to be more assertive and choose keyword to help. Repeat.

Add D3 to overload the defence.

Potential Question to Pose

What keywords will help a player to move decisively and assertively?

(Answer: Varied, for example, 'drive', 'clear', 'ball', 'mine', 'strong'.)

PRACTICE: SHOOTERS – BE STRONG
NUMBERS: FOUR

Players are asked to maintain a strong T position under increasing defensive pressure.

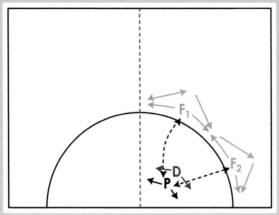

Practice Outcomes

* To use keywords and positive images to maintain T position under pressure of defence.

* To maintain a strong base to provide a good passing and shooting option.

* To adjust position according to the movement of the ball, own team and defence.

Progressions and Differentiation

D increases movement against P.

Increase movement and speed of passing between F1 and F2.

Add second D against P.

Task/Group Organization

F1 and F2 offer and reoffer for passes, using top of D and pockets particularly. Pass ball between them, looking to feed shooter when appropriate.

P holds T stance and repositions to react to movements of F1 and F2 and holds position strongly as D tries to deny P their chosen space. Repeat five times.

P visualizes strong position and chooses a keyword to help emulate the strong position. Repeat five times.

D increases efforts to deny P space, varies defensive positioning. Repeat five times.

Potential Question to Pose

How do you maintain a strong T position?

(Answer: Know where the post is, use tall, strong body position and angles to keep vision open, ready to see others.)

PRACTICE: IT'S 'MY BALL'!
NUMBERS: FOUR

Players are encouraged to use keywords to increase assertiveness when competing for a 50:50 ball.

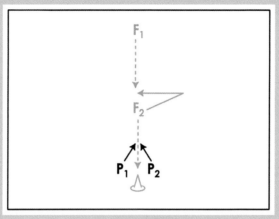

Practice Outcomes

* To increase assertiveness when going for a 50:50 ball.

* To utilize keywords to enhance performance and obtain the appropriate mindset.

* To develop different keywords to help with different aspects of performance.

Task/Group Organization

F1 starts with ball, F2 cuts out and back to receive pass from F1, as timing cue. P1 and P2 start at cone and compete for ball. P1 first, with P2 starting at 50 per cent effort and becoming increasingly competitive.

F2 gives straight-line pass to mid-line between P1 and P2. Jog recovery. Six repetitions.

Players use keywords, for example, 'mine', 'drive', 'go', which P1 shouts out first while going for the ball, then internalizes the call.

Progressions and Differentiation

Explore different keywords and manner in which they are voiced.

Vary height, speed and angle of feed.

Relate to positional contexts.

Potential Question to Pose

Which keywords help to improve assertiveness at different stages of this practice?

(Answer: For example, 'go', 'drive', 'explode' to get a fast start; 'mine', 'snatch' to take ball.)

PRACTICE: 'MY SPACE'
NUMBERS: FIVE

Players are challenged to anticipate the space they would like to move into and assertively hold the defence away from it.

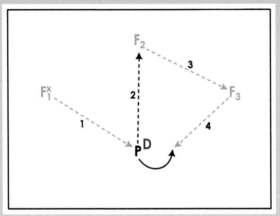

Practice Outcomes

* To read the movement of players to anticipate the space required and communicate clearly when and where the player wants the ball.

* To reposition strongly to protect that space.

* To use keywords to support the strength of hold and decisiveness of movements to receive the pass.

Task/Group Organization

F1, F2 and F3 feed ball between them – limited movement at first, gradually increasing range of movement. Each player holds onto the ball for at least 2 seconds to allow P time to position.

P positions and repositions to protect space, offers for pass. When received, returns to another feeder and resets.

Six to eight repetitions. Review how to anticipate space and movement. Choose keywords to strengthen hold.

Progressions and Differentiation

Increase movement of feeders and vary time holding on to the ball.

Adapt to specific court areas – dead-ball situations first, then more open play.

Potential Questions to Pose

What should a player look for to know which space to protect?

(Answer: Positioning of feeders and defence.)

Which keywords help performance?

(Answer: 'Strong', 'hold', then 'go'/'mine'.)

PRACTICE: DEFENCE – TALK TO EACH OTHER!
NUMBERS: THREE

Players are required to react to each other and communicate effectively to take the intercept.

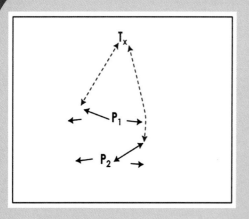

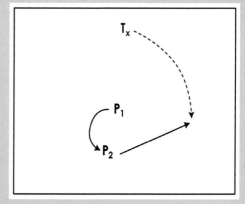

Practice Outcomes

* To keep the defensive unit mobile throughout.

* To read which pass to go for.

* To communicate clearly when going for the ball.

* To respond to a partner's positioning and switch where necessary.

* To switch and interchange positioning effectively and efficiently.

Progressions and Differentiation

Verbal shout becomes internalized.

P1 and P2 discuss how to read each other better. Change partners.

Adapt to the court area, add second feeder, then add defence.

Task/Group Organization

(a) P1 and P2 mobile within area.

T feeds in pass randomly, varies height and speed of ball.

Nearest P responds with clear shout of 'mine' when going for ball. Collects pass, returns to T and resets.

P1 and P2 react to each other's positioning – when one is pulled out of position (b), switch position and maintain movement. 8–10 repetitions.

Potential Questions to Pose

How can a player communicate effectively with their partner?

(Answer: Shout 'mine' as going for the ball.)

When should the switch take place?

(Answer: When partner is pulled out of position, fill the space left behind.)

PRACTICE: MENTAL TOUGHNESS – MANAGING 'SLEDGING' NUMBERS: EIGHT

Players are distracted during game play and challenged to regain their focus.

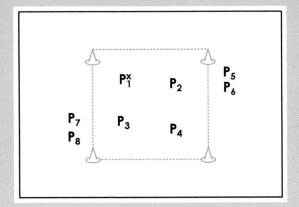

Practice Outcomes

* To practise coping with 'sledging' (personal comments made by opposition designed to distract).

* To provide distractions whilst performing (comments/heckles from other players).

* To refocus on performance as quickly as possible.

* To use keywords and concentration skills to help.

* To use relaxation and pre-performance routines before restarting.

Task/Group Organization

P1–P4 pass and move within playing area. Twelve passes, then pause.

P5–P8 provide comments relating to individual performance to put off players; vary position, volume and type of comment.

P1–P4 attempt to shut out distractions and use keyword to help refocus concentration when broken.

When paused, use breath control to relax, visualize good performance and remind self of keyword to help regain positive mindset before restarting. Repeat.

Progressions and Differentiation

Increase intensity and frequency of comments. Include comments in break.

P5–P8 become active defence, but maintain comments made to distract.

Potential Questions to Pose

Which type of distraction is most challenging?

(Answer: Varied – could include volume of comments, personal nature or proximity.)

How can a player refocus once distracted?

(Answer: Keywords to be 'here and now'.)

PRACTICE: USE PENALTIES WISELY
NUMBERS: EIGHT

Players are challenged to use a routine during a penalty to control emotions and establish a positive mindset before re-entering play.

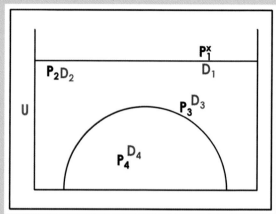

Practice Outcomes

* To develop a short routine to cope with the emotional reactions to 'bad' umpiring decisions.

* To develop player's control to:

 – remove frustration, use physical movement;

 – refocus attention, for example open up vision;

 – re-enter the game positively, for example decide what to do next.

* To reduce the time taken to control emotions and react positively to penalty decisions.

Task/Group Organization

4v4 in end third of court. P1 and P2 work as centre/wing attack and start/restart game on third line and sideline. Play through to scoring opportunity.

D1–D4 tight one-on-one, look for intercept.

Umpire calls decisions on D3, deliberately.

After four to five decisions, review D3's reaction, then choose routine to try when standing at player's side and use it during the penalty.

P3 hold ball for full 3 seconds to give D3 chance to use routine before re-entering play.

Four to five penalties called and routine practised.

Progressions and Differentiation

Reduce time player has to execute a routine.

Extend to other performers.

Use more pressure.

Potential Question to Pose

What does a player find the most helpful focus before re-entering play?

(Answer: Varied, could include 'breathe', 'look up', 'walk tall'.)

PRACTICE: LOOK–NOTICE–DELIVER NUMBERS: TEN

The centre is asked to use a pre-performance routine to open up their vision before taking the centre pass.

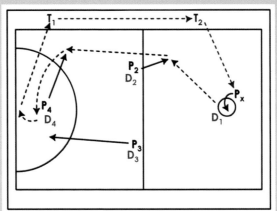

Practice Outcomes

* To give the centre a short routine to execute immediately before entering the centre circle to deliver the centre pass.

* To open up the player's vision to identify cues from both attacking and defending players.

* To support the centre to prepare herself for the next pass while recovering to the centre circle.

Progressions and Differentiation

Include P4 as well.

Vary who has hands held up. Include defence, P1 calls D first, then P.

Increase pace next ball fed in by T.

Task/Group Organization

Centre pass set up. As they set up on the line, P2 and P3 hold up arm and hand with a number of fingers extended. Vary number shown.

P1 pauses before stepping into circle to take pass, looks up and calls out number of fingers P2 and P3 hold up.

P1 then focuses on what they are about to do with the centre pass, repeats to self a keyword to help. Steps into circle and delivers. Plays through to shot at goal.

Potential Question to Pose

How can a player's routine to set up the centre pass be speeded up?

(Answer: Run back, look up as turn to see players and defenders, say keyword as step in circle and deliver.)

PRACTICE: SUBSTITUTE WELL
NUMBERS: TEN

–t Players are substituted to practise emotional control and confidence-building before coming back on court during modified game play.

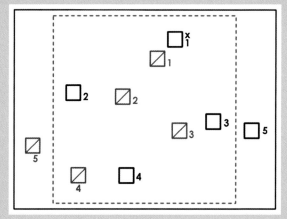

Practice Outcomes

* To use substitutions within a high-intensity small-sided game.

* To encourage players on the bench to identify their arousal levels and aim to control them – by relaxing or hyping up.

* To use best-performance imagery and positive self-statements to maintain confidence.

* To use physical activity and goal-setting to prepare to play again.

Task/Group Organization

Five players in each team, four playing, one substituted.

Two teams in different coloured bibs.

Pass in sequence, alternating colours. Pass to different player. After releasing the ball, move to outside of area before reoffering. Ten passes = one goal.

Rotate substitutes after 3 minutes.

Subs – monitor feelings on bench, use relaxation or breath control to calm or energize self if needed. Refocus on best-performance image and personal strengths, use positive keyword before re-entering play. Practise before re-entering play.

Progressions and Differentiation

Use of two balls to raise intensity and emotions when substituted.

Add third colour bib and maintain sequence. Add defence.

Potential Question to Pose

What images and self-talk can be used to achieve a positive mindset before going back on court?

(Answer: For example, think of good performance, set goal for re-entering play, use keyword to help focus on the next move. Walk tall!)

PRACTICE: COPING WITH UMPIRING DECISIONS
NUMBERS: TEN

Players practise controlling their emotional reaction to umpiring calls against them.

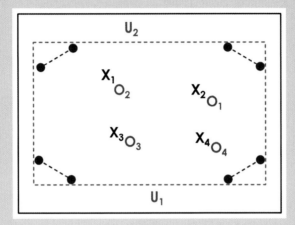

Practice Outcomes

* To experience strict umpiring and the calling of penalties for justified and manufactured reasons.

* To practise routine at a penalty and extend to a routine that can be used within free play.

* To develop stages within routine to:
  – control emotions, for example, 'breathe', use physical cue, such as wipe hand down dress;
  – open up vision – look up;
  – refocus on the 'here and now'.

Task/Group Organization

4v4 match play – varied use of goal gates to score, diagonal or same end.

Umpires pull penalties strictly on each player (manufactured if needed). Attackers take full 3 seconds to release the ball. Player uses routine when standing at side of player to gain positive mindset to re-enter game. Play for 5 minutes.

Review, adapt routine for free-pass decisions and use during free play.

Progressions and Differentiation

Reduce time player has while standing within a penalty.

Deliberately not call decisions expected so that P adapts mindset during play.

Randomize allocation of penalties and free-pass decisions, increase pressure.

Potential Question to Pose

How can a player's emotional reaction to umpiring decisions be controlled?

(Answer: Recognize decision out of P's control, use frustration as trigger to focus on what comes next.)

GLOSSARY OF
NETBALL-SPECIFIC TERMS

Advantage A term used by the umpire to signal that an infringement has occurred but play does not stop. The team in possession continues to play.

Attacking team The team in possession of the ball.

Attacking third The goal third where a team attacks the shooting circle being defended by the opposition.

Attacking unit This unit is a group of players, namely the goal shooter, goal attack, wing attack and centre, who will often set tactical strategies as a group.

Back pass When a centre player distributes the ball at the centre pass to a player behind her, which could be the goal defence or the wing defence.

Back space The area available behind the receiver to move into and receive a pass.

Ball carrier The player in possession of the ball.

Ball-side The position of a player is nearer to the ball than their opponent.

Baseline run This is where a goal shooter or goal attack will enter the circle running parallel to the goal line.

Boxing out This is where a goal defence or goal-keeper turns their back on an incoming shooter under the post to protect the space to take the rebound. Shooters can use it too.

Centre circle The circle in the mid-third where the centre must stand to take the centre pass.

Centre pass This is taken to start and also to restart the game after a goal has been scored.

Centre third The middle third on the netball court.

Circle rotation This involves the goal shooter and goal attack in the shooting circle who move to balance the circle in terms of their positioning both widthways and lengthways.

Channels A coach will often use the word to describe the imaginary divisions of the court lengthways. The left, mid and right channels are

terms used to ensure that a player is aware of the space and width available on attack.

Circle edge This is the area surrounding the shooting circle where the wing attack and centre should aim to position to support and pass to the shooters.

Clearing run A player may execute a clearing run to leave space or create a space for a teammate to move into.

Contact Netball is a non-contact sport and this means that opposing players must not physically contact each other.

Cues External factors that are visible and contribute to the decisions made.

Dead-ball situation This is where the ball has gone out of play, or an infringement has occurred on the court and play is to restart from a set position.

Defending team The team not in possession of the ball.

Defending unit This unit is a group of players, namely the goal keeper, goal defence, wing defence and centre, who will often set tactical strategies as a group.

Double lead Moving to receive the ball and then repositioning, often by changing direction to be an option for the same or next pass.

Double play A player passes the ball to the receiver, then takes the next pass.

Execution phase A skill is divided into three phases and the execution phase follows the preparation phase and is the point at which the action commences. The recovery, or follow-through, represents the final phase after the action has occurred.

External imagery This is where a player sees themselves completing a movement as if they are watching themselves on TV.

Fake or feint pass A player carries out the

preparation to throw to deceive and commit the opposition.

Falling start This is when an individual will transfer their body weight into the direction of movement from a static position.

Feeder The player repeatedly passing the ball to another player.

Focus of attention What a player is concentrating on at any point in time. This can be something within the body, internal focus, or something outside their body, an external focus. It could also be on a broad perspective, when reading the game, or a narrow focus if concentrating on a specific performance element.

Front cut A player on the attack will move in front of their opponent to receive the ball.

Front player The player nearer to the ball.

Front position A player adopts a position on the front of their opponent and is nearer to the ball.

Front space The area available in front of the individual moving to receive a pass.

Getting free The ability of a player to outwit their opponent to receive the ball.

Goal line There are two goal lines and they are situated behind the shooting circle.

Goal third There are two of these; they are the thirds that are at either end of the court containing a shooting circle.

Hidden hand When a hand remains by the side of the body and is hidden from the view of the attacker, giving a false sense of free space in which to deliver a pass.

High ball A pass that has a high trajectory.

Imagery This is when a player relives an element of performance, using as many senses as possible, without actually doing it. This can include reliving a best performance or practising something in the mind just before it is performed.

Initiator The player who will make the first move, often the player nearer to the ball.

Interception Gaining possession by cutting off a pass between two opposing players.

Internal imagery Visualizing performance by doing it in the mind, where the feelings of the movement are particularly powerful.

Keywords Single words or short phrases that players can say to themselves to simulate the movement they wish to make, or the cue on which they wish to focus their concentration.

Lead Movement to receive a pass.

Man-to-man Marking a player tightly, sometimes referred to as 1v1.

Marking Pressurizing and staying close to an opposing player, often trying to prevent them from receiving the ball or moving into a desired area of the court.

Mid-court area Refers to the centre third area of the court.

Obstruction This is when a player defends from the incorrect distance and can also occur when a player covers the path of an opposing player by using outstretched arms.

Offer The first attacking move to receive, often called a lead.

Offside This is called by the umpire when a player enters into a playing area they are not allowed to move into.

Off the ball This refers to an action by a player or players that occurs when they are not in possession of the ball, or the immediate person to receive a pass.

Options Refers to the number of players who are in a suitable position to receive the ball.

Outcome goals A target set to beat the opposition or to be the best.

Overlapping player This is a player who moves from behind play to position at the side or ahead of the ball carrier to receive the ball.

Patterns of play The movement of players and pathway taken of the ball through the court to the goal.

Perceptual factors The external factors that need to be considered when executing a skill.

Peripheral vision The width and depth that a player is able to see.

Performance goals A target set to monitor a specific element of performance that can be measured, such as shooting averages.

Pivot When an individual keeps their landing foot planted on the ground and moves to face another direction using the non-landing foot.

Pre-performance/shot routine A series of stages that players can take to be secure and confident in their preparation of performance.

Preliminary move A move often used to clear space before the attacking move to receive is executed.

Pressure on the ball The second stage of defence.

PRIDE This is where a player sets themselves an individual target to support their team's efforts. Stands for Personal Responsibility In Delivering Excellence.

Process goals A target set to help players to focus on a specific element of technique or tactic.

Protecting a space A player may mark a player and

keep them away from the space in which they want to receive the ball.

Rebound An individual gains possession after an unsuccessful attempt at goal.

Re-offer Another move to receive the ball if the lead or first offer is not successful or used.

Repositioning Movement to find another space or position on the court, or to be in the best position in relation to an opponent.

Restrictive marking Used to prevent a player from taking off immediately after a pass and the defender will angle their body to prevent the attacker moving in the direction they wish.

Roll An attacking skill, in which a player changes direction by rolling off their player.

Screen Where a player protects a space for a fellow teammate to move into.

Set-up This refers to the position of players and often relates to their starting position at a throw-in or centre pass.

Shooter One of the two players who can score a goal and enter the shooting circle (goal shooter and goal attack).

Shuffling Small sidesteps in various directions, used to reposition often when defending a player.

Sledging Personal comments made by the opposition, designed to distract players.

Square pass The ball carrier delivers the ball to a player at their side.

Stack This describes the set-up of two players, often

the goal attack and wing attack, at the centre pass who position one in front of the other on the third line.

Straight-line pass The ball carrier distributes a pass to a player directly on a straight line in front of them.

Switching This is where two players may remain in the same position but change roles temporarily, for example the centre position and wing attack might do this when the ball is in the centre third. The wing attack moves ahead of the centre and does more work in the mid-court area, allowing the centre to drop into the goal third.

Take-off This is the first step taken when moving from a stationary position.

Throw-in When the ball lands on the ground outside of the court a throw-in is taken to bring the ball back into play.

Tip When a player touches the ball in an uncontrolled manner with the fingertips.

Tracking Following an opponent's movements, or following the movement of the ball when defending.

Transition Changing from one phase of defence to another, or attack to defence.

Triggers Use of cues in the environment to stimulate players to control when and where they react; these can be visual, auditory or verbal.

Turnover When the defending team gains possession from the attacking team.

INDEX